ERRATUM

EXPLORING THE REASONS BEHIND
THE NARROWING GENDER GAP IN EARNINGS

by Elaine Sorensen

The correct title of chapter two is:

Why Women's Relative Pay Increased in the 1980s

EXPLORING THE REASONS BEHIND THE NARROWING GENDER GAP IN EARNINGS

URBAN INSTITUTE REPORT 91–2

Elaine Sorensen

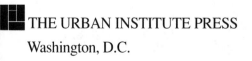

THE URBAN INSTITUTE PRESS

Washington, D.C.

THE URBAN INSTITUTE PRESS
2100 M Street, N.W.
Washington, D.C. 20037

Exploring the Reasons Behind the Narrowing Gender Gap in Earnings / Elaine Sorensen.

1. Wages--Women--United States. 2. Equal pay for equal work--United States. 3. Women--Employment--United States. I. Title. II. Series.

HD6061.2.U6S68   1991   90-26783
331.4'2153'0973--dc20   CIP

(Urban Institute Reports; 91-2 ISSN 0897-7399)

ISBN 0-87766-507-9
ISBN 0-87766-506-0 (casebound)

Printed in the United States of America.

Distributed by University Press of America

4720 Boston Way	3 Henrietta Street
Lanham, MD 20706	London WC2E 8LU
	ENGLAND

URBAN INSTITUTE REPORTS are designed to provide rapid dissemination of research and policy findings. Each report contains timely information and is rigorously reviewed to uphold the highest standards of policy research and analysis.

The Urban Institute is a nonprofit policy research and educational organization established in Washington, D.C., in 1968. Its staff investigates the social and economic problems confronting the nation and government policies and programs designed to alleviate such problems. The Institute disseminates significant findings of its research through the publications program of its Press. The Institute has two goals for work in each of its research areas: to help shape thinking about societal problems and efforts to solve them, and to improve government decisions and performance by providing better information and analytic tools.

Through work that ranges from broad conceptual studies to administrative and technical assistance, Institute researchers contribute to the stock of knowledge available to public officials and private individuals and groups concerned with formulating and implementing more efficient and effective government policy.

Conclusions or opinions expressed in Institute publications are those of the authors and do not necessarily reflect the views of other staff members, officers or trustees of the Institute, advisory groups, or any organizations that provide financial support to the Institute.

ACKNOWLEDGMENTS

The study on which this report is based was funded by the U.S. Department of Labor (DOL) under contract number 99-8-042-75-066-01. The views expressed in this report are those of the author and do not necessarily reflect the positions of DOL or the Urban Institute. I would like to thank Don Chiavacci, a Research Analyst at DOL, for his support throughout this project. I would also like to thank Lee Bawden, Director of the Human Resources Policy Center at The Urban Institute, who has offered much encouragement over the years for my research. I further appreciate the first-rate job of computer programming by Dar Hay and Neal Jeffries, former employees of The Urban Institute. Finally, I would like to extend a special appreciation to Michael Walker, also a former employee of The Urban Institute, who assisted in the later phases of this project with remarkable insight and enthusiasm.

CONTENTS

List of Tables and Figures

ABSTRACT

This study has three objectives. The first objective is to determine what factors contributed to the improvement in women's relative pay in the 1980s. The second objective is to analyze the potential of high-wage, high-growth jobs for increasing women's relative pay. The third objective is to provide a more in-depth analysis of a single factor previously thought to influence women's relative pay, namely, women's intermittent labor force participation. Among a number of factors that contributed to the rise in women's relative pay, the most salient factor was the change in the occupational characteristics of male and female workers. Other factors that contributed to the narrowing of the male-female pay differential included: (1) a decline in labor market discrimination against women; (2) a rise in the relative quality of female labor; and (3) a convergence in the industrial distribution of male and female workers.

EXECUTIVE SUMMARY

This study looks at the major factors influencing future trends in women's relative pay. The 1980s witnessed a dramatic rise in the relative pay of female workers. In 1988, women working full-time and year-round earned 66 percent as much as men working full-time and year-round, up from 59 percent 10 years earlier. This dramatic rise contrasts sharply with the 1960s and 1970s, when the female-male pay ratio hovered around 59 percent. Some analysts have projected that this pay ratio will continue to rise during the 1990s, reaching 74 percent by the year 2000. But the forces behind these momentous changes have not been examined.

Among a number of factors that contributed to the rise in women's relative pay, the most salient factor was the change in the occupational characteristics of male and female workers. Other factors that contributed to the narrowing of the male-female pay differential included: (1)

a decline in labor market discrimination against women; (2) a rise in the relative quality of female labor; and (3) a convergence in the industrial distribution of male and female workers. Since all of these factors are likely to continue to change in a favorable manner for women, the prospects for further improvements in women's relative pay are good.

Most high-wage, high-growth jobs are found in three broad occupational categories: managerial, professional, and technical. The following five areas of work dominate this list: health, computers, engineering, teaching, and general management. The skill requirements of these jobs have been found to be considerably higher than the skill requirements of the average job in the U.S. economy.

This study also finds that today's young women are more likely than previous young women to have the requisite characteristics for high-wage, high-growth jobs. For example, they have acquired more education and more wage-enhancing education than young women in the past. However, despite these improvements, there are still differences between the characteristics of today's young women and young women before them who later entered high-wage, high-growth jobs. For instance, this latter group of women exhibited even greater investments in education than today's young women exhibit. Today's young women have taken fewer mathematics courses in high school, have lower educational goals, and are less likely to have finished four years of college than young women before them who later entered high-wage, high-growth jobs.

Over 85 percent of the female workforce between the ages of 35 and 41 have worked intermittently. These women earn 30 percent less than women in this age group who have worked continuously. This study finds that most of this pay differential is due to differences in characteristics between these two groups of women. For example, half of the women who work continuously do not have children; only 12 percent of other women in this age group have remained childless. It is also estimated, however, that continuous female workers earn significantly more than intermittent female workers even after controlling for productivity differences. Almost 40 percent of the pay differential is unexplained by productivity differences.

1

INTRODUCTION

OBJECTIVES AND SIGNIFICANCE OF STUDY

The purpose of this study is to understand the major factors that may influence future trends in women's relative pay. The 1980s witnessed a dramatic rise in the relative pay of female workers. In 1988, women working full-time and year-round earned 66 percent as much as men working full-time and year-round, up from 59 percent 10 years earlier. This dramatic rise contrasts sharply with the 1960s and 1970s, when the female-male pay ratio hovered around 59 percent. Some analysts have projected that this pay ratio will continue to rise during the 1990s, reaching 74 percent by the year 2000. But the forces behind these momentous changes have not been examined.

Specifically, this study has three objectives. The first objective is to determine what factors contributed to the improvement in women's relative pay in the 1980s. The second objective is to analyze the potential of high-wage, high-growth jobs for increasing women's relative pay. The third objective is to provide a more in-depth analysis of a single factor previously thought to influence women's relative pay, namely, women's intermittent labor force participation.

Each of these basic objectives is further divided into various subobjectives. The first objective initially examines the trends in women's relative pay. It then describes the explanations previously given for its recent improvement, and a research method is developed to test the merits of these explanations. The second objective initially determines which jobs offer women high-wage, high-growth opportunities. It then analyzes the characteristics of the women who already hold these positions. Finally, it presents an intercohort comparison between young women today and young women 14 years earlier who later chose high-wage, high-growth jobs. The third objective examines the role of intermittent labor force participation by developing a bivariate probit model of women's earnings that distinguishes between women who work intermittently and women who work continuously. This model is then estimated and the earnings disparity between continuous and intermittent female workers is examined.

Why the male-female pay differential declined during the 1980s is an important policy question, as well as an interesting economic question, for several reasons. First, policymakers would like to know whether women's relative pay improved because of a decline in employer discrimination against women. If sex discrimination in the labor market has not declined, this calls into question the effectiveness and relevance of existing antidiscrimination policies. Second, although projections have been made regarding the future trends in women's relative pay, these projections have been based upon previous trends rather than underlying causes, yielding unrealistic predictions of women's relative pay. A more reliable method uses the underlying causes of previous change to predict future trends in women's relative pay. If future improvements are expected to continue at this rapid rate, a substantial redistribution of earnings between male and female workers will result, which is bound to have serious repercussions both in and outside of the labor market.

Policymakers also need to know the extent to which women can be expected to meet the projected demand for skilled workers in managerial, professional, and technical positions. The U.S. Bureau of Labor Statistics (1988) has predicted that 40 percent of job growth between 1988 and 2000 will occur in these three occupational categories. Between 1970 and 1988, women filled 60 percent of the new jobs in these fields. Can female workers be expected to continue to fill the majority of these positions? These occupational categories are the only ones that offer women both above-average earnings and above-average employment growth. Thus, one way to increase male-female pay equality is for women to continue taking advantage of the increased job opportunities in these fields. This study provides information about the attitudes, educational attainment, and employment decisions of women already employed in high-wage, high-growth fields. This information is useful in determining strategies for young women who would like to enter higher-wage jobs.

Finally, a basic difference between male and female workers has been their commitment to the labor force. Men have tended to work continuously; women have tended to work intermittently. Many economists have argued that this difference is a key reason why women earn less than men. This study contributes to the ongoing research in this area by examining the labor market behavior and outcomes of continuous and intermittent female workers. It sheds light on the role of intermittent labor force participation in maintaining the earnings disparity between women and men.

OUTLINE OF STUDY AND SUMMARY OF FINDINGS

This report is divided into four chapters. This first chapter describes the study's objectives and outlines the study's findings. Chapter 2 examines why women's pay relative to men's pay improved in the 1980s. Chapter 3 describes which jobs offer women above-average earnings and above-average projected growth rates to the year 2000, referred to as well-paid, high-growth ("hipaygrow") occupations in this report. It then examines the characteristics of women aged 35 to 41 who currently hold these positions and presents an intercohort comparison between young women today and young women 14 years earlier who later chose high-wage, high-growth jobs. Chapter 4, the final chapter, examines whether labor force intermittence explains why women who work continuously earn significantly more than women who work intermittently. A summary of the findings for each of these research components follows.

Using data from the University of Michigan's 1984 Panel Study of Income Dynamics (PSID), chapter 2 examines why women's pay relative to men's pay increased during the 1980s. One explanation is cited as standing out among the others, namely, that during this period the occupational characteristics of male and female workers converged. The study also finds that two other factors helped explain why the male-female pay differential narrowed during the 1980s: (1) the quality of female labor improved relative to that of male labor; and (2) labor market discrimination against women declined. Although the industrial distribution of male and female workers converged during this period, the overall effect of changes in the industrial characteristics of workers did *not* contribute to the rise in women's relative pay, casting doubt on the argument that industrial restructuring was a leading factor in the narrowing of the male-female pay differential.

Chapter 3 uses data from the U.S. Bureau of Labor Statistics, the U.S. Bureau of the Census, and the *Dictionary of Occupational Titles* (the latter summarized in Miller et al. 1980) to determine which jobs offer women above-average earnings and above-average projected employment growth rates to the year 2000. It finds that most high-wage, high-growth jobs are in three broad occupational categories--managerial, professional, and technical--with five areas of work dominating this list: health, computers, engineering, teaching, and general management. The skill requirements of these jobs are reviewed and found to be considerably higher than those of the average job in the U.S. economy.

Data from the National Longitudinal Survey (NLS) of Young Women (ages 14-24 in 1968) are then used to examine the characteristics of women aged 35 to 41 who hold high-wage, high-growth positions. These women are found to have invested in education significantly more than other working women. They had stronger educational goals at an early age, took more mathematics courses while in high school, selected more wage-enhancing college majors, and stayed in school longer.

The last part of chapter 3 presents an intercohort comparison of young women between the ages of 23 and 29, using data from the NLS of Youth (ages 14-21 in 1979) and Young Women. It examines the characteristics of young women in this age group in 1973 and 1987. It also describes the characteristics of a subgroup of the women in 1973 who later chose a high-wage, high-growth job, and compares them to the characteristics of young women today. This analysis finds that today's young women, on the whole, are acquiring more human capital and more wage-enhancing human capital than young women of the past. However, despite these improvements, there are still differences between the characteristics of today's young women and young women from 14 years earlier who now work in high-wage, high-growth jobs. This latter group of women exhibited even greater investments in human capital than today's young women exhibit.

Chapter 4 uses the NLS of Young Women to examine why a pay differential exists between women who work continuously and women who work intermittently. This disparity may or may not be due to mean differences in characteristics between these two groups of women. This analysis uses a bivariate probit selectivity model to estimate earnings equations for continuous and intermittent female workers. It finds that women who work continuously earn 50 percent more than women who work intermittently, but that most of this pay differential is due to differences in characteristics between continuous and intermittent female workers. It is estimated, however, that the hourly pay of a woman who works intermittently would increase by 17 percent if she worked continuously, explaining 38 percent of the total pay differential between these two groups of women.

2

WHY WOMEN'S RELATIVE PAY INCREASED IN THE 1990S

WHY WOMEN'S RELATIVE PAY INCREASED IN THE 1980S

Women's relative pay improved substantially during the 1980s. From 1978 to 1989, the median weekly salary of full-time female workers increased from 61 percent to 70 percent that of full-time male workers. This chapter examines the reasons for this. First, to highlight these recent trends, background information is given on the relative pay of women over time. Then, alternative explanations for why women's relative pay increased in the 1980s are discussed. Finally, original research is presented that evaluates the relative merits of these explanations.

TRENDS IN THE MALE-FEMALE
PAY DIFFERENTIAL

Two data series, illustrated in figure 2.1, are often used to compare male and female earnings. The first series measures women's median *annual* pay as a percentage of men's median *annual* pay for full-time, year-round workers. This series has been published annually since 1955, when it equaled 64 percent (U.S. Bureau of the Census). During the next five years it fell to 59 percent, where it hovered for the next two decades. In 1981, it was still 59 percent, but since then it has steadily increased to 66 percent. The second series--the ratio of female to male median *weekly* pay for full-time workers--shows a similar pattern for the years that it is available, but this ratio is typically 2 to 4 percentage points higher than the first one (U.S. Bureau of Labor Statistics, *Employment Earnings*, various issues). By 1989, this ratio equaled 70 percent, up from 61 percent in 1978.

There are two basic differences between these two series. First, the annual series measures pay for a more restricted sample of workers--they must work full-time and year-round--whereas the weekly series applies only to those who work full-time. Second, the number of hours a person works affects both measures of pay, but it affects the first series more, since hours can vary over the week as well as over the year in this series. Men work more hours per week and more weeks per year on average than women. Since both of these factors affect the annual figure, this series tends to report a lower pay ratio than the weekly figure.

Figure 2.1   RATIO OF FEMALE TO MALE EARNINGS
FOR FULL-TIME WAGE AND SALARY
WORKERS

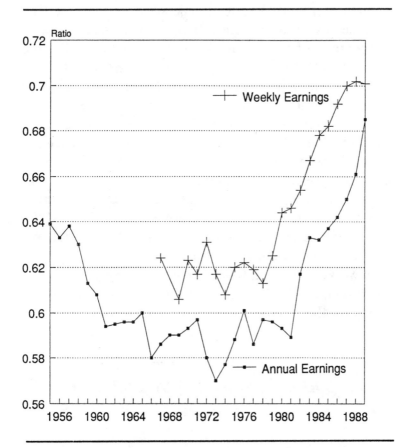

Sources: U.S. Bureau of Labor Statistics, *Employment and Earnings*, various issues. U.S. Council of Economic Advisors, *Economic Report of the President*, 1987. U.S. Bureau of the Census, "Money Income and Poverty Status in the United States" P-60 series, various issues.

Note: Annual earnings are for full-time and year-round workers.

Figure 2.2 illustrates two other measures of women's relative pay over time. Both of these measures were developed using data from the Panel Study of Income Dynamics (PSID), described in detail in appendix A. The first series reports women's median *hourly* pay as a percentage of men's median *hourly* pay for full-time workers. This measure completely eliminates the influence of differences in hours between women and men, providing a more accurate description of women's relative pay than either of the two previous series. The second measure is the same as the first, except that all workers are included in this ratio, not just full-time workers. The first series focuses upon full-time workers rather than all workers, to limit the impact of varying hours on earnings. But examining hourly pay already eliminates this variation. Thus, the PSID series can be used to assess whether women's relative pay improved in the 1980s for all workers, not just full-time workers. Indeed, figure 2.2 shows that the hourly pay of women relative to that of men increased during the 1980s for all workers, including full-time workers.

REASONS GIVEN FOR THE INCREASE IN WOMEN'S RELATIVE PAY

The following five explanations have been given for the narrowing of pay disparity between the sexes during the 1980s:

Figure 2.2   RATIO OF FEMALE TO MALE MEDIAN
             HOURLY EARNINGS

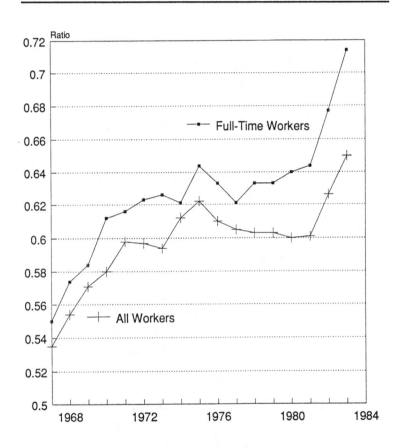

Source: University of Michigan, Panel Study of Income Dynamics,
1984.

1. The quality of female labor improved relative
    to that of male labor, contributing to the rise in
    women's relative pay. It is already known, for
    example, that the actual work experience of the
    average female worker increased in the 1980s
    relative to that of the average male worker. It is
    suggested that this improvement contributed to
    the gain in women's relative pay.

2. The narrowing of the male-female pay differen-
    tial in the 1980s may be attributed to a decline
    in labor market discrimination against women.
    Although no major antidiscrimination legisla-
    tion was passed during this period, it may be
    that earlier legislation and executive orders as
    well as changing attitudes among employers
    resulted in the improvement in women's rela-
    tive pay.

3. The industrial distribution of employment
    shifted in the 1980s away from unionized,
    energy-intensive, and foreign-trade-sensitive
    industries, owing, in part, to the oil shock of
    1979, the back-to-back recessions in 1980-82,
    and the overvaluation of the dollar in the 1980s.
    This restructuring of the economy may have
    negatively affected male workers more than
    female workers, thus contributing to the rise in
    women's relative pay.

4. The wage premiums previously available to
    male workers in certain sectors of the economy,

such as unionized firms, declined during the 1980s for the same reasons as described in explanation number 3. These changes may have contributed to the narrowing of the male-female pay differential.

5. The occupational distribution of male and female workers may have converged over time, contributing to the increase in the relative pay of women. This convergence may be caused by many different factors: for instance, it may reflect an improvement in women's unmeasured productivity characteristics; or a shift in labor demand; or a decline in employment discrimination.

PREVIOUS EMPIRICAL RESEARCH

Previous research has examined the first four of these explanations, but as is described here, the studies employed data inadequate to analyze this issue, thus vitiating their results. Hypothesis number 5, although as yet unresearched, may prove to be the strongest explanation for why women's relative pay increased in the 1980s.

The earliest research (e.g., Smith and Ward 1984) on why women's relative pay improved in the 1980s focused upon the first explanation. This research asserted that the productivity-related characteristics of male and female workers converged during the 1980s, explaining all of the rise in women's relative pay. More recent research has examined whether changes in the demand for labor have contributed to the narrowing of the male-female pay differential. Blau and Beller (1988) have argued that the second hypothesis, declining labor market discrimination against women, was a primary factor leading to the rise in women's relative pay. Other authors, reporting on more recent research, have contended that other demand factors, such as increased foreign competition, have altered the labor market, resulting in higher relative pay for female workers (Bound and Johnson 1988). The following paragraphs describe these and other studies in more detail.

Smith and Ward (1984), who were the first to examine why the relative pay of female workers increased in the 1980s, argued that the wages of working women did not rise relative to those of working men between 1920 and 1980 because the skill of working women did not rise relative to that of men over this period. However, they claimed that the increase in women's relative pay since 1980 *does* reflect an increase in the relative skill of female workers. Although these hypotheses are reasonable, the authors never tested them. They showed that between 1920 and 1980 the level of education and work experience of female workers did not increase relative to that of male workers, but they did not illustrate how this affected the relative pay of women. Instead, they estimated a model of female wage growth as a function of male wage growth, without ever examining the factors that influenced male wages. They found that between 1950 and 1980, female workers received a 56 percent increase in pay for every 100 percent increase in male wages. But this result does not tell us *why* women's pay remained around 56 percent of men's pay for most of this period. An analysis of why relative wages change must examine the factors affecting both male and female wages.

The next paper published on this topic was by Blau and Beller (1988), who asserted that women's relative pay increased between 1971 and 1981 because of declining gender role specialization and declining discrimination. They estimated earnings equations for women and men (by race) for 1971 and 1981, with and without a selection correction, and found that white women's relative pay increased by 15 percent over this decade. This gain was then broken into two parts: that which was due to changes in means and that which was due to changes in coefficients. The authors used the latter component to measure whether a decline in discrimination contributed to the rise in women's relative pay. They found that among whites, changes in the means and coefficients contributed about equally to the decline in the gender pay differential.

There are two limitations to this latter research approach. First, the researchers used Current Population Survey (CPS) data, which do not include measures of actual work experience. Potential work experience (i.e., age minus education minus six) is used as a proxy for actual work experience, but this measure probably underestimates the convergence between the mean years of men's and women's actual work experience. Second, the authors' earnings equations do not include union status or industrial characteristics of the workforce, so they cannot address the merits of the third and fourth hypotheses, which argue that the U.S. economy has undergone restructuring that has negatively affected male earnings more so than female earnings.

Levy (1988) and others have argued that women's pay has increased relative to men's pay because of a shift in the economy away from goods-producing industries toward the service sector. This argument is related to an important question that received considerable attention during the 1980s, that being whether the U.S. economy is still producing "good jobs," a term generally referring to jobs that offer middle-class incomes to individuals with a high school education (Blackburn, Bloom, and Freeman 1990). Many analysts are concerned that the economy is no longer generating sufficient numbers of these jobs, and is instead generating high-paying jobs requiring a great deal of skill or extremely low-paying jobs requiring no skill, despite the fact that most workers fall in between these two extremes (Johnston 1987).

Some of these authors have pointed to a number of factors that have accelerated this shift in employment since 1979, including the oil shock of 1979, the back-to-back recessions of 1980-82, the overvaluation of the dollar during the 1980s, and the declining unionization of the workforce. These events, it is argued, have negatively affected male workers more than female workers because the former are more likely to work in unionized, energy-intensive, recession-sensitive, and foreign-trade-sensitive industries (Levy 1988). Furthermore, these industries have tended to pay higher wages than other industries, even after taking into account productivity characteristics. Thus, as male workers move out of these industries into lower paying ones, their average earnings will decline relative to female earnings.

There is clear evidence that women's pay increased relative to men's pay, and that industrial employment shifted in the 1980s, but the existence of these two trends does not necessarily mean that one caused the other. Despite Levy's

(1988) assertions of such a link, there is scant empirical research to support it. Most of the research in this connection has, in fact, examined males exclusively (Blackburn et al. 1990; Murphy and Welch 1988), but implications are drawn from these findings about why women's relative pay increased during this period.

Bound and Johnson (1988) are the only authors who have tried to examine this issue using an appropriate analytic design. They tested two basic hypotheses, that: (1) shifts in industry demand have led to the rise in women's relative pay; and (2) shifts in wage premiums paid by particular industries have resulted in higher relative pay for women. The authors found little empirical backing for either hypothesis. At the same time, an unfortunate weakness of this paper is that it uses CPS data, which lack detailed measures of labor quality.

In summary, a number of hypotheses have been put forth to explain why women's relative pay has improved, including a convergence in labor quality, a decline in discrimination, a shift in the industrial distribution of employment, and a shift in the wage premiums paid by particular industries. Although all of these authors allude to the importance of the first hypothesis, none of them adequately test it, primarily because they have relied on CPS data, which do not include adequate measures of actual work experience. Since labor quality is never precisely measured, these authors' estimates of the impact of industrial shifts, changes in wage premiums, and changes in discrimination also lack certainty.

Finally, none of the existing studies of why women's relative pay rose in the 1980s examine the impact of the changing occupational distribution of male and female workers, which, it should be emphasized, has changed at least as much as workers' industrial distribution. Popular literature has certainly pointed to this change as the motivating factor behind the rise in women's relative pay (Bernstein 1988). Nevertheless, this hypothesis has not been empirically examined.

RESEARCH METHOD

This section endeavors to surmount the weaknesses in data and methodology of the existing research examining why women's relative pay increased in the 1980s. The research method I use evaluates the merits of the five preceding explanations for why women's relative pay improved, by estimating separate earnings equations for male and female workers in 1979 and 1984. The change in the earnings disparity between women and men is then calculated and decomposed into several components, using an extension of the Oaxaca method (1973). This decomposition can be explained as follows.

To examine what factors influence the male/female earnings disparity, economists typically first estimate separate earnings equations for male and female workers. The following two equations describe this effort:

$$\ln w_m = X_m A_m \qquad (2.1)$$

$$\ln w_f = X_f A_f, \qquad (2.2)$$

where: m and f represent male and female workers, respectively; $\ln w$ is the logarithm of hourly wages; X is a vector of characteristics thought to influence earnings; and A is a vector of estimated coefficients for these characteristics.

The mean difference in male and female earnings is then divided into two parts: (1) that due to mean differences in characteristics and (2) that due to differences in estimated coefficients. This decomposition can be achieved as follows:

$$\overline{\ln w_m} - \overline{\ln w_f} =$$
$$\overline{X}_m - \overline{X}_f) A_m + \overline{X}_f (A_m - A_f), \tag{2.3}$$

where: $\overline{\ln w}$ represents the mean of the logarithmic wage; and $\overline{X}$ represents a vector of mean values for the explanatory variables.[1]

To simplify the notation, this equation can also be written as:

$$G = \Delta \overline{X} A_m + \overline{X}_f \Delta A, \tag{2.4}$$

where: G is the total male-female pay gap; $\Delta \overline{X} = (\overline{X}_m - \overline{X}_f)$; and $\Delta A = (A_m - A_f)$.

The second component of this decomposition, the differences in estimated coefficients, is used by many economists as an estimate of labor market discrimination against women (Cain 1986). It measures the portion of the male-female disparity that is not explained by mean differences in productivity characteristics, that is, the pay disparity that remains between male and female workers who have the same productivity characteristics.

Others have pointed out, however, that this estimate of labor market discrimination may actually overestimate or underestimate labor market discrimination. On the one hand, certain productivity characteristics remain unobserved in any analysis. If men, on average, are more favorably endowed with these omitted characteristics than women, this component will overestimate labor market discrimination. On the other hand, some of the control variables in the regression analysis may be affected by discrimination. Thus, including these factors leads to an underestimate of labor market discrimination. This research is not immune to the problem of estimating discrimination. Hence, this component is referred to here as the unexplained portion of the male-female pay differential, or the residual, and is attributed both to employer discrimination and differences in unmeasured characteristics. This section does not seek to resolve this debate, but to estimate whether this factor and others have contributed to the decline in the total male-female pay disparity.

The decline in the total male-female pay gap between one year, say year t, and another year, say year t', can be written as:

$$G_{t'} - G_t = (\Delta \overline{X}_{t'} \, A_{mt'} +$$
$$\overline{X}_{ft'} \, \Delta A_{t'}) - (\Delta \overline{X}_t \, A_{mt} + \overline{X}_{ft} \, \Delta A_t). \tag{2.5}$$

Rearranging terms, this can be rewritten as:

$$G_{t'} - G_t = (\overline{X}_{ft'} \Delta A_{t'} - \overline{X}_{ft} \Delta A_t) +$$
$$(\Delta \overline{X}_{t'} A_{mt'} - \Delta \overline{X}_t A_{mt}) . \tag{2.6}$$

This means the decline in the male-female pay differential between times t and t' can be divided into two parts: (1) that due to a decline in the residual, or unexplained portion of the pay gap; and (2) that due to a decline in the mean differences in male and female characteristics.

The second term in this decomposition, $(\Delta \overline{X}_{t'} A_{mt'} - \Delta \overline{X}_t A_{mt})$, measures the mean difference in male and female characteristics at time t and t'. However, the mean difference for each year is weighted by a different set of estimated coefficients. The mean difference at time t is weighted by the estimated coefficients from the male earnings equation at time t. Similarly, the estimated coefficients from the male earnings equation at time t' are used as the weights for time t'. Hence, this second term measures the change in the mean differences between male and female characteristics *and* the change in the male earnings structure. These two effects can be measured separately by further dividing the second term into the following:

$$(\Delta \overline{X}_{t'} A_{mt'} - \Delta \overline{X}_t A_{mt}) =$$
$$(\Delta \overline{X}_{t'} - \Delta \overline{X}_t) A_{mt} + (\Delta \overline{X}_{t'} \Delta A_m) . \tag{2.7}$$

Now the first term of this decomposition measures the convergence between male and female characteristics using the same weight, A_{mt}. The second term measures the extent to which the decline in the male-female earnings gap is due to a change in the male earnings structure.[2]

To summarize, the decline in the total pay gap can be divided into the following three parts:

$$G_{t'} - G_t = (\overline{X}_{ft'} \, \Delta A_{t'} - \overline{X}_{ft} \, \Delta A_t) +$$
$$(\Delta \overline{X}_{t'} - \Delta \overline{X}_t) A_{mt} + (\Delta \overline{X}_{t'} \, \Delta A_m) \, . \tag{2.8}$$

These three terms assess the relative merits of the explanations for why women's relative pay increased as follows:

1. The first term measures the extent to which a decline in the residual has contributed to the rise in women's relative pay. This measures the change in labor market discrimination and a convergence among unobserved productivity characteristics. Thus, it examines the merits of the second explanation given earlier--that labor market discrimination has declined, contributing to the rise in women's relative pay.

2. The second term measures the extent to which a convergence between the characteristics of male and female workers has contributed to the decline in the male-female pay differential. This term determines whether the labor quality of female workers has improved relative to male workers. It also shows whether the occupational and industrial distribution of male and female workers has converged over time. Thus, this term will shed light on the first, third, and fifth explanations given earlier for why women's relative pay increased.

3. The third term measures the extent to which a change in the male earnings structure has contributed to the rise in women's relative pay, testing the fourth hypothesis given earlier that rates of returns for certain characteristics have declined for male workers more than female workers, thus contributing to the rise in women's relative pay.

Finally, the rise in women's relative pay is examined here based on the total effect of changes resulting from the different types of explanatory variables in the analysis. This delineation enables one to determine the extent to which any particular variable (or set of variables) contributes to the rise in women's relative pay. For example, the relative contribution of the total change in industrial employment, including changes in means and coefficients, is assessed.

EMPIRICAL ESTIMATIONS

Data from the Panel Study of Income Dynamics (PSID) are used to estimate separate earnings equations for women and men in 1979 and 1984. The dependent variable is log hourly earnings for civilian, nonagricultural, non-private-household wage and salary workers who are at least 18 years old. The sample includes 1,964 women and 2,332 men in 1979, and 2,392 women and 2,709 men in 1984. The names and definitions of the independent variables included in this analysis are given in table 2.1, and table 2.2 reports the mean values for these variables.

The estimated coefficients for these regressions are presented in table 2.3. These findings are similar to those of previous empirical research on earnings. Most of the estimated coefficients for the productivity characteristics, for example, are lower for female workers than male workers. Similarly, the three key productivity variables--years of education completed, years of actual work experience, and years of employer tenure--have increased over time for women and men. Among the demographic characteristics, the dummy variable that equals one for those who are black has a negative estimated coefficient for both black women and men, and its absolute value has increased over time. In other words, the pay disparity between black and white workers increased during the 1980s, even after controlling for productivity-related characteristics. Other empirical research has found similar results (Vroman 1989). The marital and fertility status of male and female workers does not have a significant effect on earnings.

A series of dummy variables is included in these earnings equations that reflect a person's region, union status, industry, and occupation. There are three dummy variables--Northeast, North Central, and West--that equal one if a worker lives in that part of the country. The omitted region is the South. Most of the estimated coefficients are significantly positive, meaning that workers earn significantly more in these regions as compared to the South. Workers in the North Central portion of the country, however, are the least likely to earn significantly more than workers in the South. The estimated coefficients for the union dummy variable, which equals one if a worker is working under a union contract, are significantly positive for both male and female workers in both years.

There are 27 industry dummy variables that equal one if a worker is employed in a particular two-digit Standard Industrial Classification (SIC) code. The omitted industry is personal services. The estimated coefficient for public administration, for example, is .252 (with a standard error of .053) for women in 1979, which means that in 1979 female workers were estimated to earn 25 percent more in public administration than in personal services after controlling for productivity-related characteristics. It is interesting to note that the estimated coefficients for the durable manufacturing industries, such as transportation equipment, have increased over time for male and female workers.

Finally, there are five occupation dummy variables that equal one if the worker is employed in a particular one-digit Standard Occupational Classification (SOC). The five dummy variables are: craft, repair, and precision produc-tion occupations (i.e., skilled blue collar); operative and laborer occupations (i.e., unskilled blue collar); profes-sional and technical occupations; management and manage-ment-related occupations; and clerical and sales occupa-tions. The omitted occupational category is service work. These estimated coefficients tend to be significantly posi-tive; the obvious exception are the estimated coefficients for unskilled blue-collar work, which are insignificant for male and female workers in both years. All of the esti-mated coefficients for the occupation dummy variables declined over the period 1979-84 for male workers. In contrast, the estimated coefficients for these variables have increased for female workers, except for the estimated

Table 2.1 VARIABLE NAMES AND DEFINITIONS

Variable	Definition
Productivity Characteristics	
Education	Number of years of schooling completed
Actual work experience	Number of years employed
Home-time	Age minus actual work experience minus education minus 5
Tenure	Number of years worked for current employer
Work experience squared	Actual work experience squared
Home-time squared	Home-time squared
Tenure squared	Tenure squared
Full-time	1 if individual usually worked at least 35 hours per week during the previous year; zero otherwise
Demographic Characteristics	
Black	1 if black; zero otherwise
Hispanic and others	1 if Hispanic or other minority; zero otherwise
Married	1 if married; zero otherwise
Divorced	1 if divorced; zero otherwise
Number of children	Number of children under age 18 in the home
Youngest child under age three	1 if there is a child under three in the home; zero otherwise

Variable	Definition
Demographic Characteristics *(continued)*	
Youngest child under age six	1 if there is a child under age six in the home; zero otherwise
Youngest child age six or older	1 if there is a child at least age six years old in the home; zero otherwise
Regional Characteristics	
North Central	1 if lives in North Central region; zero otherwise
Northeast	1 if lives in Northeast region; zero otherwise
West	1 if lives in West; zero otherwise
Industrial Characteristics	
Union contract	1 if covered by a union contract; zero otherwise
Agriculture through professional services	27 dummy variables that equal 1 if employed in the relevant two-digit Standard Industrial Classification (SIC) code; zero otherwise
Occupational Characteristics	
Unskilled blue-collar to clerical and sales	5 dummy variables that equal 1 if employed in the relevant one-digit Standard Occupational Classification (SOC) code; zero otherwise

Source: University of Michigan, Panel Study of Income Dynamics, 1984.

Table 2.2 WEIGHTED MEANS OF DEPENDENT AND
INDEPENDENT VARIABLES INCLUDED IN
EARNINGS EQUATIONS

Variable	1979		1984	
	Females	Males	Females	Males
Salary (natural log)	1.505	2.017	1.885	2.287
Education	12.685	12.729	12.875	12.871
Actual work experience	11.516	19.326	12.163	20.107
Home-time	8.861	2.027	7.918	1.861
Tenure	4.644	6.842	4.851	6.537
Work experience squared	224.205	527.307	228.385	562.291
Home-time squared	164.545	12.916	138.778	11.504
Tenure squared	51.108	107.459	53.447	98.950
Full-time	.758	.969	.730	.931
Black	.119	.077	.125	.082
Hispanic and others	.030	.031	.034	.034
Married	.654	.829	.637	.791
Divorced	.211	.072	.205	.082
Number of children	.928	1.089	.846	.918
Youngest child under age three	.069	.106	.069	.099
Youngest child under age six	.092	.123	.111	.116

Variable	1979		1984	
	Females	Males	Females	Males
Youngest child six or older	.340	.324	.296	.267
North Central	.279	.321	.247	.297
Northeast	.225	.226	.244	.216
West	.203	.170	.194	.190
Union contract	.180	.342	.183	.276
Agriculture	.006	.022	.004	.026
Mining	.001	.012	.002	.012
Construction	.009	.095	.011	.091
Metal	.011	.045	.012	.036
Machinery	.046	.070	.054	.075
Transportation equipment	.016	.077	.011	.056
Food	.008	.023	.006	.023
Tobacco	.002	.002	.003	.002
Textile	.045	.016	.026	.011
Paper	.002	.006	.003	.008
Print	.016	.025	.020	.020
Chemical	.012	.036	.010	.033

Table 2.2 *(Continued)*

Variable	1979		1984	
	Females	Males	Females	Males
Transportation	.014	.057	.014	.051
Communications	.019	.024	.019	.030
Finance	.073	.031	.083	.033
Business services	.022	.030	.027	.041
Medical services	.163	.028	.168	.035
Educational services	.179	.070	.173	.065
Other durables	.017	.055	.016	.046
Misc. manufacturing	.011	.014	.015	.014
Public administration	.068	.082	.072	.078
Utilities	.009	.030	.010	.036
Wholesale trade	.022	.029	.020	.025
Retail trade	.138	.071	.135	.094
Other trade	.003	.005	.005	.002
Entertainment	.003	.007	.002	.007
Professional services	.052	.031	.054	.036
Unskilled blue collar	.124	.240	.113	.224
Skilled blue collar	.018	.283	.013	.234
Professionals	.213	.198	.239	.218
Managers	.078	.159	.084	.162
Clerical and sales	.397	.084	.389	.089

Source: University of Michigan, Panel Study of Income Dynamics, 1984.

Table 2.3 LOG EARNINGS REGRESSION RESULTS, 1979
AND 1984 (standard errors in parentheses)

	1979		1984	
Variable	Females	Males	Females	Males
Intercept	.450*	.271	.726*	.344*
	(.079)	(.125)	(.085)	(.107)
Education	.041*	.049*	.043*	.062*
	(.005)	(.005)	(.005)	(.005)
Actual work experience	.011*	.026*	.018*	.034*
	(.003)	(.003)	(.003)	(.003)
Home-time	-.003	-.012	-.004	-.004
	(.003)	(.006)	(.003)	(.006)
Tenure	.012*	.020*	.019*	.015*
	(.003)	(.003)	(.003)	(.003)
Work experience squared	-2.E-04*	-5.E-04*	-4.E-04*	-6.E-04*
	(7.E-05)	(6.E-05)	(7.E-05)	(6.E-05)
Home-time squared	2.E-05	2.E-04	1.E-06	-2.E-04
	(8.E-05)	(2.E-04)	(1.E-04)	(3.E-04)
Tenure squared	-3.E-04	-5.E-04*	-5.E-04*	-3.E-04*
	(1.E-04)	(1.E-04)	(1.E-04)	(8.E-05)
Full-time	.102*	.177*	.090*	.129*
	(.020)	(.048)	(.020)	(.034)
Black	-.048	-.074	-.079*	-.107*
	(.025)	(.032)	(.025)	(.031)
Hispanic and others	.056	-.030	.018	.017
	(.047)	(.048)	(.045)	(.046)

Table 2.3 *Continued*

Variable	1979		1984	
	Females	Males	Females	Males
Married	-.006	.072*	.007	.049
	(.026)	(.033)	(.025)	(.032)
Divorced	-.010	.053	.035	.068
	(.030)	(.041)	(.029)	(.039)
Number of children	-.010	-.004	-.003	-.026
	(.011)	(.011)	(.013)	(.013)
Youngest child	.007	.023	-.040	.096
under age 3	(.038)	(.038)	(.041)	(.041)
Youngest child	-.005	-.023	-.027	.090
under age six	(.036)	(.036)	(.037)	(.041)
Youngest child six	.026	-.002	4.E-05	.030
or older	(.028)	(.029)	(3.E-02)	(.032)
North Central	.026	.059*	-.015	.039
	(.021)	(.022)	(.022)	(.022)
Northeast	.031	.075*	.066*	.095*
	(.023)	(.024)	(.022)	(.024)
West	.065*	.143*	.098*	.118*
	(.024)	(.026)	(.023)	(.025)
Union contract	.162*	.132*	.129*	.181*
	(.022)	(.019)	(.023)	(.021)
Agriculture	.023	-.077	-.115	.095
	(.107)	(.101)	(.142)	(.090)

Variable	1979		1984	
	Females	Males	Females	Males
Mining	.488	.301*	.298	.542*
	(.330)	(.112)	(.168)	(.105)
Construction	.250*	.313*	.219	.370*
	(.090)	(.089)	(.089)	(.079)
Metal	.456*	.318*	.326*	.283*
	(.086)	(.093)	(.087)	(.087)
Machinery	.398*	.282*	.318*	.435*
	(.059)	(.090)	(.060)	(.080)
Transportation equipment	.480*	.293*	.569*	.453*
	(.075)	(.090)	(.090)	(.082)
Food	.233	.230	.274	.231
	(.095)	(.100)	(.115)	(.092)
Tobacco	.499*	.197	.635*	.759*
	(.172)	(.209)	(.159)	(.192)
Textile	.139	.048	.060	.145
	(.063)	(.105)	(.073)	(.108)
Paper	.398	.230	.223	.324*
	(.175)	(.136)	(.142)	(.117)
Print	.226*	.249	.054	.378*
	(.075)	(.098)	(.074)	(.094)
Chemical	.317*	.315*	.485*	.428*
	(.083)	(.094)	(.093)	(.086)

Table 2.3 *Continued*

Variable	1979		1984	
	Females	Males	Females	Males
Transportation	.278*	.272*	.395*	.326*
	(.077)	(.091)	(.082)	(.083)
Communications	.369*	.249	.414*	.437*
	(.071)	(.100)	(.075)	(.088)
Finance	.196*	.235	.145	.383*
	(.053)	(.095)	(.057)	(.086)
Business service	.152	.148	.152	.136
	(.066)	(.096)	(.067)	(.084)
Medical services	.210*	.125	.227*	.235*
	(.046)	(.097)	(.052)	(.085)
Educational services	.084	-.034	.048	-.025
	(.048)	(.090)	(.054)	(.081)
Other durables	.192	.209	.203	.310*
	(.077)	(.092)	(.080)	(.083)
Misc. manufacturing	.278*	.276	.014	.261*
	(.084)	(.108)	(.081)	(.101)
Public admin-istration	.252*	.151	.278*	.271*
	(.053)	(.089)	(.057)	(.080)
Utilities	.371*	.240	.112	.412*
	(.095)	(.096)	(.091)	(.086)
Wholesale trade	.222*	.206	.180	.265*
	(.067)	(.096)	(.074)	(.090)

Variable	1979		1984	
	Females	Males	Females	Males
Retail trade	-.007	.054	-.075	.091
	(.047)	(.089)	(.053)	(.078)
Other trade	.242	.117	-.027	.029
	(.143)	(.141)	(.118)	(.218)
Entertainment	.252	.398*	.299	.310*
	(.143)	(.127)	(.170)	(.119)
Professional services	.162*	.123	.066	.164
	(.055)	(.097)	(.059)	(.086)
Unskilled blue collar	.011	.110	.012	.003
	(.039)	(.049)	(.039)	(.039)
Skilled blue collar	.128	.249*	.253*	.168*
	(.064)	(.049)	(.074)	(.039)
Professionals	.341*	.427*	.372*	.314*
	(.031)	(.050)	(.030)	(.039)
Managers	.349*	.543*	.415*	.346*
	(.036)	(.051)	(.037)	(.040)
Clerical and sales	.101*	.191*	.148*	.112*
	(.026)	(.053)	(.026)	(.043)
Adjusted R^2	.450	.482	.496	.528
Sample size	1964	2332	2392	2709

Source: University of Michigan, Panel Study of Income Dynamics (PSID), 1984.

Note: Asterisk (*), significant at the 1 percent level (two-tailed tests).

coefficient for unskilled blue-collar work, which remained insignificant at .01 (with a standard error of .04).

DECOMPOSING THE GAIN IN WOMEN'S RELATIVE PAY

In 1979, the mean logarithmic earnings for male and female workers were 2.017 and 1.505, respectively. These figures increased to 2.287 and 1.885 respectively, in 1984. Hence, the mean differential between the logarithmic earnings of male and female workers declined by .11, from .512 in 1979 to .402 in 1984. This means that women's relative pay increased by 12 percent during these five years, from a pay ratio of .60 to .67.[3]

Table 2.4 presents the decomposition of the male-female pay gap. It should be remembered that this table decomposes the *decline* in the pay differential. Thus, any factor with a negative sign contributed to the decline, and any factor with a positive sign did not contribute to the decline. The table's columns include the three components of the decomposition described in the research method, dividing the total decline into: (1) that due to a decline in the residual; (2) that due to a convergence in the mean characteristics; (3) that due to a decline in the male earnings structure. The rows represent groups of variables (or a single variable) included in the earnings regressions. The table shows, for example, that the union status of male and female workers converged during 1979-84 (-.009 out of

Table 2.4 DECOMPOSITION OF DECLINE IN MALE-FEMALE PAY DIFFERENTIAL, 1979-84

	Due to Changes in:			
Groups of Variables[a]	Residual	Mean	Male Earnings Structure	Total
Intercept	-.204	0	0	-.204
Productivity Characteristics	.144	-.023	.032	.153
Demographic Characteristics	-.012	.0002	-.004	-.016
Regional Characteristics	-.011	.002	-.001	-.010
Union Status	.015	-.009	.005	.011
Industrial Characteristics	.112	-.014	.009	.107
Occupational Characteristics	-.119	-.014	-.019	-.152
Total	-.074	-.057	.021	-.110

Source: University of Michigan, Panel Study of Income Dynamics, 1984.

a. Productivity characteristics include education, actual work experience and its square, tenure and its square, home-time and its square, and full-time status; demographic characteristics include race/ethnic dummy variables, marital status dummy variables, and fertility measures; regional characteristics include three dummy variables for regions in the country; union contract is a dummy variable that equals one if the individual is covered by a union contract; industrial characteristics are 27 dummy variables representing two-digit SIC codes; occupational characteristics are 5 dummy variables representing one-digit SOC codes. See tables 2.1 and 2.2 for more detail.

-.110), but the total effect of this factor did *not* contribute to the decline in the male-female pay differential, since changes in the other components, namely, the residual (.015 out of -.110) and the male earnings structure (.005 out of -.110), were larger and positive.

Table 2.4 shows that the quality of female labor did increase relative to male labor, explaining about 20 percent of the decline in the male-female pay differential (-.023 out of -.110). Hence, this study finds support for the first explanation given earlier, that the rise in women's relative pay was due in part to a rise in the relative quality of female labor. But it also shows that the change in the residual (.144) and the male earnings structure (.032) for these variables more than offset this convergence. This part of the residual increased sharply because the male estimated coefficients for these variables increased much more than the female estimated coefficients. Between 1979 and 1984, for example, the estimated coefficient for education increased from .049 to .062 for men, but it only increased from .041 to .043 for women. In other words, male workers went from a 5 percent to a 6 percent rate of return for each additional year of education over this period, but the rate of return for female workers hardly increased at all. Other research has found similarly dramatic increases in the returns owing to education in the 1980s (Murphy and Welch 1988). This research confirms these results, but it also goes one step further and shows that women's returns to education have not increased as rapidly as men's. Hence, these large changes in the estimated coefficients for productivity characteristics mean that the *total* effect of changes in productivity characteristics did not contribute to the narrowing of the male-female pay differential.

Similar results are found for the industrial characteristics as well. Table 2.4 shows that the industrial distribution of employment for male and female workers converged between 1979 and 1984, explaining about 10 percent of the decline in the male-female pay differential (-.014 out of -.110), but it also shows that the residual and the male earnings structure component increased for these characteristics. Again, the men's estimated coefficients for these variables increased more than the women's. For example, the men's estimated coefficient for construction increased from .313 to .370, whereas the women's decreased from .250 to .219. These figures indicate that after controlling for other characteristics, men working in the construction industry earned over 30 percent more than men in personal services. Furthermore, this wage differential increased over time. In contrast, the wage differential between construction and personal services for female workers was initially around 25 percent, and it declined over time. At the same time, men's employment decreased in the construction industry, while women's employment increased. Thus, even though more women were represented in this industry, the total effect of changes in the industry did not contribute to the decline in the male-female pay differential. This pattern of diverging coefficients between male and female workers is true for almost all of the two-digit industries included in this analysis. It is most striking in the durable manufacturing industries where employment for men declined but the estimated coefficients for men rose.

Table 2.4 also shows that overall changes in the male earnings structure did *not* contribute to the decline in the male-female pay differential. Although the estimated coefficients for some characteristics declined over this period, the sharp rise in the estimated coefficients for male productivity characteristics overshadowed these changes. Interestingly enough, the estimated coefficients for union status and traditionally male industries, such as durable manufacturing, construction, and transportation, rose for men during the 1980s, even though male employment in these areas declined. Hence, this study finds no support for the fourth explanation given earlier, that the rise in women's relative pay could be attributed to changes in the male earnings structure.

This study finds evidence, however, to support the second explanation given earlier, that a decline in labor market discrimination against women has contributed to the decline in the male-female pay differential. Table 2.4 shows that the residual declined sharply over this period (-.074 out of -.110), suggesting that either sex discrimination decreased or that changes in unmeasured productivity characteristics contributed to the decline in the male-female pay differential. Since the total effect of changes in *measured* productivity characteristics did not contribute to the narrowing of the pay differential, it suggests that the changes in *unmeasured* characteristics did not contribute to the reduction in the residual either, leaving a decline in sex discrimination as the most likely explanation for the decline in the residual.

Finally, table 2.4 demonstrates that one set of variables contributed more than any other to the rise in women's relative pay, namely, the change in the occupational characteristics of workers. Not only did the occupational distribution of male and female workers converge during this period, explaining about 10 percent of the total decline in the male-female pay differential, but for these variables, the other components (the residual and male earnings structure) decreased as well. Table 2.3 reveals that all of the estimated coefficients for these variables declined for men, but they uniformly rose for women. Although it is true that the male estimated coefficients for blue-collar work declined, this was not an isolated phenomenon. For example, the estimated coefficient for management occupations declined for men as well, from .543 to .346, but it rose for women, from .349 to .415. Thus, in 1979, men working as managers earned over 50 percent more than men working in service occupations even after controlling for productivity-related characteristics. But in 1984, this wage differential declined to 35 percent. For women, the wage differential rose from 35 to 42 percent. Thus, these results suggest that wage differentials are converging across occupations for men, once productivity characteristics and the type of industry are controlled for, but they are diverging for women.

This finding--that wages have converged between women and men within broad occupational categories but have diverged within broad industrial categories--is somewhat surprising. I had expected to find that economic restructuring had caused pay to converge both within occupations and industries. This unexpected result may be due to the specification of the earnings equation, which uses 27 dummy variables to characterize different industries but only 5 dummy variables to characterize different occupations. It may be that an equal number of occupation and industry dummy variables would have produced different results. Moreover, it may be more appropriate to view occupation as an endogenous variable that is affected by the distribution of industrial employment. In this case, adding occupation dummy variables to an ordinary least-squares

regression may yield misleading results. These other speci-
fications should be explored in future research on this
subject.

In summary, this research finds empirical support for
four of the five explanations given earlier for the rise in
women's relative pay, but one of these stands out among
the others, that women's relative pay rose because of the
changes in the occupational characteristics of male and
female workers. Not only did the occupational distribution
of male and female workers converge over time, but the
rates of returns to occupations converged as well. This
study also finds support for the first and second explanations given earlier, that the rise in women's relative pay can
be attributed to a rise in the relative quality of female labor
and a decline in the labor market discrimination against
women. Finally, it shows that the industrial distribution of
male and female workers has converged over time, lending
support to the third explanation given earlier that women's
relative pay rose in part because of industrial changes in
employment. But the total effect of changes in the industrial characteristics of male and female workers did not
contribute to the decline in the male-female pay differential, arguing against the industrial restructuring position.
Finally, the study finds no support for the fourth argument,
that changes in the male earnings structure reduced the
relative earnings of men.

Notes, chapter 2

1. The weights applied to each of these terms, A_m and $\overline{X}_f$,
are arbitrary. They could just as easily have been A_f and $\overline{X}_m$.

This is often referred to as the index problem. I selected the first set of weights because this compares the average female wage with the wage women would have received if they had the same estimated earnings function as men.

2. In order to see that the term $(\Delta \overline{X}_t, \Delta A_m)$ measures the amount of the decline in the male-female pay differential that can be attributed to a change in the male earnings structure, suppose the male earnings structure applies to both male and female workers. In such a case, the decline in the pay differential between times t and t' would be equal to $(\Delta \overline{X}_t, A_{mt'} - \Delta \overline{X}_t A_{mt})$, the term on the left-hand side of equation (2.7). Hence, a decline in the male-female pay differential could be due to a convergence in gender characteristics or a change in the male earnings structure. If the male earnings structure did not change, then the pay differential would equal $(\Delta \overline{X}_t' - \Delta \overline{X}_t) A_{mt}$. The difference between these two scenarios, $(\Delta \overline{X}_t, \Delta A_m)$, determines the extent to which a change in the male earnings structure contributes to a decline in the male-female pay gap.

3. The following formula gives this percentage change:

$$.116 = e^{.11} - 1.$$

hours, in job location near home and limited out-of-town travel insofar as they often cite the demands of their families.

Perhaps the most illuminating example often cited to demonstrate the ways in which women deemphasize their work life is that women tend to leave the labor market to accept the role of mother while the children are young. These interruptions tend to lower their earnings because their skills deteriorate during their time out of the labor force, and because they are not willing to take a new job in the place to obtain earnings to the extent workers might. Intermittent labor market attachment can also adversely affect the necessary human capital accumulation underlying earnings.

Corcoran, Duncan, and Ponza (1984), who were among the first to look into this behavior of work histories, showed their results and found that age when women reentered the labor market after raising children, and due to differences in work experience.

3

WELL-PAID, HIGH-GROWTH JOBS FOR WOMEN: WHAT ARE THEY, WHICH WOMEN ENTER THEM, AND WHY?

The latest labor force projections to the year 2000 predict that the U.S. labor force will grow more slowly than in the recent past (Fullerton 1989). Another 19 million people are expected to be added to the U.S. labor force between 1988 and 2000, at an annual growth rate of 1.2 percent. In contrast, during the past 12 years, 25 million people were added to the labor force at a 2 percent annual rate. This slower growth will be due in part to the slower growth in the population over the age of 15, which is expected to increase at an annual rate of less than 1 percent. The other major factor affecting labor force trends is the labor force participation rate, which measures the percentage of the population over 15 years old currently in the labor force. This rate is expected to rise 3 percentage points between 1988 and 2000, from 66 percent to 69 percent, but this is a smaller increase than during the past 12 years when the rate increased 4 percentage points, from 62 to 66 percent. This slowing down of the growth in the labor force participation rate is anticipated because of the changes in the demographic composition of the labor force.

The demographic composition of the labor force is expected to change dramatically between 1988 and 2000. Women are expected to represent nearly two-thirds of the labor force growth between now and the year 2000, at which time 47 percent of the labor force is expected to be female. The labor force is also expected to grow older over the next decade as the baby-boom generation (those born between 1946 and 1964) grows older. By 2000, this group will be 35 to 54 years old and will represent nearly 50 percent of the labor force. This age group currently represents only 40 percent of the labor force. Finally, the U.S. labor force is expected to include a greater share of minority groups in the year 2000. Blacks, Hispanics, and Asians are expected to represent 26 percent of the labor force by that time, up from 21 percent in 1988.

The occupational distribution of the American labor force is also expected to change (Silvestri and Lukasiewicz 1989). The three major occupational groups requiring the highest levels of educational attainment--managerial, professional, and technical--are projected to grow more rapidly than the average 15 percent predicted for all occupations over the 1988-2000 period. More than 40 percent of all new jobs created during this period will be in one of these three categories. The only other broad occupational groups that are expected to have above-average employment growth are sales and service work, both of which currently have a median level of educational attainment among their workforce, namely 12.8 years. All of the other occupational categories--administrative support, craft and repair, operative and laborer, and farming--are growing slower than average, and none requires more than the median level of education. Hence, it is predicted that new jobs created over the period 1988-2000 will require substantially more education than is currently expected of workers.

WELL-PAID, HIGH-GROWTH OCCUPATIONS FOR WOMEN

Given these anticipated changes in the labor force, the question is: Where are the employment opportunities that offer women above-average earnings and above-average employment growth rates ("hipaygrow" jobs)? These occupations are listed in table 3.1.[1] Not surprisingly, most of them are in managerial, professional, or technical fields. There are no service, operative, or laborer occupations that offer women both above-average earnings and above-average employment growth rates. Furthermore, only a small number of hipaygrow jobs are in sales, administrative support, or craft and repair occupations. A brief description of these "hipaygrow" jobs follows, by occupation.[2]

Managerial Occupations

Most managerial occupations are expected to offer women above-average earnings and employment growth, and thus qualify as hipaygrow occupations. Many of these occupa-

Table 3.1 OCCUPATIONS WITH ABOVE-AVERAGE
GROWTH RATES AND ABOVE-AVERAGE
EARNINGS FOR WOMEN

Managerial Occupations
    Financial managers
    Personnel managers
    Managers, medicine
    Marketing, advertising, and
      public relations managers
    General managers
    Accountants
    Underwriters
    Other financial officers
    Management analysts
    Personnel specialists
    Business agents
    Other management

Professional Occupations
    Architects
    Engineers, metallurgical
    Engineers, civil
    Engineers, industrial
    Engineers, agricultural
    Engineers, marine
    Engineers, mechanical
    Engineers, n.e.c.
    Computer systems analysts
    Operations analysts
    Actuaries
    Statisticians
    Mathematical scientists,
      n.e.c.

Physical scientists, n.e.c.
Biological scientists
Physicians
Dentists
Veterinarians
Optometrists
Podiatrists
Health practitioners, n.e.c.
Nurses
Pharmacists
Dietitians
Occupational therapists
Physical therapists
Speech therapists
Teachers, elementary
  school
Counselors, educational
Economists
Psychologists
Sociologists
Urban planners
Social workers
Lawyers
Judges
Authors
Technical writers
Musicians
Actors and directors
Dancers
Editors

Public relations specialists Announcers--radio and television	Administrative Support Occupations Clerical supervisors
Technical Occupations Clinical laboratory technologists Dental hygienists Health record technologists Radiologic technicians Electrical technicians Engineering technicians, industrial Engineering technicians, mechanical Engineering technicians, n.e.c. Computer programmers Other technical	Sales Occupations Insurance sales Real estate agents and brokers Securities and financial services sales Advertising and related sales Travel Agents Craft and Repair Occupations Bus mechanics Aircraft mechanics Data processing equipment repairs Drywall installers Structural metal workers

Sources: Outlined in appendix A.

tions are expected to increase because of the expanding complexity of business operations. In addition, since most of the employment gains are expected to be in trade and service industries, where small firms are more prevalent, management positions are expected to represent a larger-than-average proportion of employment. Thus, the job of general manager and top executive, for example, is expected to offer more job opportunities than almost any other hipaygrow occupation, adding almost a half million positions between 1988 and 2000. Another reason for the large employment gains in this group can be traced to the large employment gains anticipated in certain industries. For example, the finance and insurance industries are expected to have above-average growth between 1988 and 2000; thus, occupations in these industries that offer women above-average earnings, such as underwriters, financial managers, and other financial officers, are included as hipaygrow occupations.

Most managerial jobs are hipaygrow jobs, with a few exceptions. For example, employment of purchasing managers is expected to grow more slowly due to computerization of purchasing tasks. Furthermore, public sector administrators are expected to expand less rapidly than other jobs, since this sector is expected to grow more slowly than the overall economy.

Despite these increases in managerial occupations, the field's overall growth rate is projected to be substantially lower than during the past 12 years, when almost 5 million new managerial occupations were added to the economy. In contrast, between 1988 and 2000, managerial occupations are expected to expand by only 2.7 million positions. Thus, the explosion of managerial jobs experienced in the past 12 years is expected to be tempered somewhat between 1988 and 2000. This may affect the number of people who select business as their college major in the future. (In 1984, over half of all students enrolled in college selected business as their college major [U.S. Bureau of Census 1987]).

Professional Occupations

The number of workers in professional occupations is projected to grow by 3.5 million between 1988 and 2000, at an annual growth rate of 2 percent a year. More than two-thirds of these jobs are hipaygrow occupations. In fact, the professional occupation group offers more hipaygrow job opportunities than any other broad occupational group. The largest hipaygrow occupations in this group are: health-related occupations, teachers (except at the college and university levels), engineers, computer specialists, and lawyers.

Employment for health professionals is expected to add more jobs to the ranks of professional workers than any other line of work, adding about 1 million jobs by 2000. The demand for health services is projected to remain strong in the future, causing this industry to grow more rapidly than industries as a whole. This will mean above-average employment growth for all workers in this industry, including its professional staff. Registered nursing, a hipaygrow job, is expected to have more openings than any other professional occupation in the health industry, adding 613,000 positions (an increase of 39 percent) between 1988 and 2000. The demand for registered nurses is expected to remain strong in part because of the need to contain costs, which encourages hospitals and other health providers to assign nurses some of the duties previously performed by doctors. The hipaygrow job with the next largest increase in employment in this field is that of physician, which is expected to increase by 150,000 positions (28 percent) between 1988 and 2000. But the hipaygrow occupation with the highest growth rate in this area is physical therapist, which is expected to increase by 57 percent between 1988 and 2000, adding about 40,000 new positions.

Two other hipaygrow job areas, those of engineers and computer specialists, are expected to add another 610,000 jobs between 1988 and 2000. The demand for engineers is expected to remain strong, in part because firms will continue to update and expand their product designs as they try to remain competitive. Among the engineering professions, electrical engineers are projected to have the largest employment gain (176,000) and the most rapid increase (40 percent). Most of this increase is expected to occur in industries such as communications equipment, computers, and other electronics equipment manufacturing. Computer specialists are expected to fill 260,000 new positions as the use of computers continues to expand among businesses. These occupations not only provide a large number of new positions, but they also have one of the highest growth rates among the professional occupations (52 percent). It should be noted, however, that the field of computer specialists includes such occupations as computer systems analysts and operations research analysts, not computer programmers. Computer programmers are included under technical occupations, discussed later.

Although the growth rate among teachers is expected to be only slightly above average for total employment, these occupations offer more hipaygrow job opportunities than most other lines of work. The number of elementary and secondary school teachers, for example, is projected to grow 17 percent between 1988 and 2000, 2 percentage points above the average for all jobs, and adding over 400,000 positions. Teachers are expected to experience above-average increases in employment because school enrollments are expected to rise, owing to the increase in births beginning in the late 1970s from the "echo" effect of the baby boom generation.

Finally, employment for lawyers is expected to grow by 31 percent, adding 181,000 positions between 1988 and 2000, reflecting the strong demand for legal services projected for this period.

Technical Occupations

Most of the technical occupations qualify as hipaygrow occupations. Occupations with the largest representation are those of computer programmer, engineering technician, legal assistant, and health technician (except for licensed practical nurse). These four types of technicians are expected to add 331,000 new positions between 1988 and 2000, capturing about three-quarters of the new technical jobs. These technical positions are in the same areas as the professional occupations already discussed; the only professional occupation missing here is that of teaching, but technicians are not generally used in this area (teacher aides and educational assistants are classified as administrative support staff). Thus, the same changes in demand and technology discussed with regard to the professional occupations apply here as well.

Among these hipaygrow occupations, health technicians are expected to have the largest employment growth, adding 337,000 new jobs (34 percent) between 1988 and 2000. The number of licensed practical nurses is expected to increase by 37 percent, adding 229,000 jobs to the workforce between 1988 and 2000 and representing the largest employment increase for a single health technician job. But because these jobs do not offer women above-

average earnings, they are not considered a hipaygrow occupation. The job of radiologic technologist, on the other
hand, is a hipaygrow occupation and is expected to have the
largest employment growth (87,000) as well as the highest
growth rate (66 percent) among the health-related technical
occupations. Computer programmers are predicted to have
the next largest increase among the technical occupations,
adding 250,000 occupations by the year 2000 (an increase
of 48 percent). Engineering technicians are expected to increase by 204,000 (28 percent) during this period. Finally,
legal assistants are expected to have the highest growth rate
of any technical occupation, increasing by 75 percent and
adding 62,000 positions.

Administrative Support Occupations

The only administrative support occupation that qualifies as
a hipaygrow job is clerical supervisor. Most administrative
support occupations are expected to grow more slowly than
the national average, but a few have above-average growth
rates. Most of these, however, do not offer women above-
average earnings. For example, occupations such as recep-
tionist, computer operator, and teacher's aide are expected
to have above-average growth rates between 1988 and
2000, but do not offer women above-average earnings.
Other occupations, such as secretary, bank teller, and tele-
phone operator, are projected to have below-average
growth rates.

Sales Occupations

Sales occupations, in general, are projected to increase by 20 percent between 1988 and 2000, adding 2.6 million new positions. Most of these occupations, however, are not hipaygrow jobs. For example, the largest occupation in this group is retail salesworker, which is projected to grow 19 percent between 1988 and 2000, adding 730,000 new jobs, but this occupation is not a hipaygrow job. In fact, only about 10 percent of the new jobs in this area are expected to offer women both above-average earnings and above-average growth rates. These include travel agents, real estate agents and brokers, and securities and financial services salesworkers.

Craft, Repair, and Precision Production Occupations

The craft, repair, and precision production occupations are projected to grow more slowly than the national average between 1988 and 2000. Furthermore, relatively few new hipaygrow positions in this area are expected to be added during this period. Precision production jobs are the hardest hit, with a 1 percent projected growth rate. Hence, no precision production job qualifies as a hipaygrow job. Although mechanics and repairers are expected to fare slightly better, they, too, are predicted to grow more slowly than the national average. Only three of these jobs--bus mechanics, aircraft mechanics, and data processing equipment repairers--are expected to offer women both above-average growth and above-average earnings. But these three jobs are expected to add only 105,000 new positions between 1988 and 2000. Craft positions, on the other hand, are expected to grow as fast as the national average between 1988 and 2000, but only two of these jobs, drywall installers and structural metal workers, qualify as hipaygrow jobs. They are expected to add only 40,000 new positions between 1988 and 2000.

Ten Well-Paid, High-Growth Jobs with the Largest Predicted Job Growth

Table 3.2 reports the ten hipaygrow occupations with the largest job growth between 1988 and 2000. These ten occupations are expected to add about 3.3 million new positions by 2000, representing about 90 percent of all hipaygrow jobs that are expected to be added to the economy during this period. There are seven broad occupational groups represented in this table: health, education, engineering, computers, legal services, accounting, and general management. The largest occupation is that of teacher (except college), which is expected to increase by 776,000 positions by 2000, an increase of 18 percent. Registered nurse, the second occupation listed, is expected to add 613,000 new positions during this period, increasing by 39 percent. Physicians are listed last on this table; they are expected to increase by 149,000 positions, which is a 28 percent increase. General managers are the third occupation, with an expected increase of 479,000 jobs, a 16 percent increase. Two computer-oriented occupations are listed, computer systems analysts and computer programmers. They are expected to increase by 214,000 (53 percent) and 250,000 (48 percent), respectively. There are also two engineering jobs, engineers and engineering tech-

Table 3.2 TEN HIPAYGROW OCCUPATIONS WITH LARGEST PROJECTED JOB GROWTH AND THEIR SEX COMPOSITION

Occupations	1988 Employment (in thousands)	Change in Employment by 2000 (in thousands)	Percentage Female in 1970	Percentage Female in 1988
Teacher (except college)	4,250	776	70	73
Registered nurse	1,577	613	97	95
General manager	3,030	479	17	39
Engineer	1,411	351	2	7
Computer programmer	519	250	23	32
Computer systems analyst	403	214	15	30
Accountant	963	211	26	50
Engineering technician	722	204	6	14
Lawyer	582	181	5	19
Physician	535	149	9	20

Sources: Silvestri and Lukasiewicz (1989); U.S. Bureau of Labor Statistics (1989); U.S. Bureau of the Census (1972).

nicians, which are expected to increase by 25 percent (351,000 positions) and 28 percent (204,000 positions), respectively. Finally, there are lawyers, who are expected to increase by 181,000 jobs (31 percent), and accountants, who are expected to increase by 211,000 positions (22 percent).

The two hipaygrow jobs with the largest expected growth are registered nurse and teacher, the only occupations on this list that are currently held primarily by women (i.e., 70 percent or more of the employees in these occupations are female). About one-third of the growth in hipaygrow jobs is expected to be in these two jobs. If women continue to fill most of these positions as they have in the past, this will offset reductions in occupational segregation by sex made elsewhere in the economy. On the other hand, well over half of the growth in hipaygrow jobs will be in jobs not traditionally held by women. If women continue to increase their share of these jobs as they have in the recent past, then occupational sex segregation among managerial, professional, and technical positions will decline. Table 3.2 reports the percentage of women in each of the 10 hipaygrow occupations in 1970 and 1988. These figures show that the percentage of women has increased in the 8 occupations not held primarily by women. Four of these occupations--physicians, lawyers, engineers, and engineering technicians--are still held primarily by men (i.e., women represent 20 percent or less of the workers in these occupations), but women have more than doubled their share of these positions in the past 18 years. The other four occupations--accountants, general managers, computer systems analysts, and computer programmers--are already integrated occupations (i.e., women hold between 20 and 70 percent of the jobs). The proportion of women holding these positions has also increased during the past 12 years.

Educational and Training Requirements of Well-Paid, High-Growth Jobs

The general education and specific training requirements of all jobs and of hipaygrow jobs in the U.S. economy are reported in table 3.3.[3] It shows that the average job requires 12 years of education and 2 years of specific training. In contrast, 14 years of education and 3 years of specific training are required for hipaygrow jobs. The skill requirements are so much greater among hipaygrow jobs because these jobs are mainly managerial, professional, or technical occupations, which require considerably more training than other jobs. Table 3.3 shows that professional occupations, for example, require 16 years of education and 4 years of specific training.

CHARACTERISTICS OF WOMEN IN WELL-PAID, HIGH-GROWTH OCCUPATIONS

What are the attributes of women in well-paid, high-growth (hipaygrow) occupations? How do these women differ from those in other occupations or from women who have decided not to work outside the home? To answer these questions, the National Longitudinal Survey (NLS) of Young Women was examined. This survey was selected because it is a longitudinal file that includes a large array of

Table 3.3   EDUCATION AND TRAINING REQUIRE-
MENTS OF ALL JOBS COMPARED TO THOSE
OF HIPAYGROW JOBS

	All Jobs		Hipaygrow Jobs	
	Years of General Education	Years of Specific Training	Years of General Education	Years of Specific Training
Average	*12*	*2*	*14*	*3*
Occupational Categories				
Managerial	14	4	14	4
Professional	16	4	16	4
Technical	14	2	14	2
Sales	12	1	13	1
Administrative				
support	12	1	12	1
Service	10	.4	--	--
Farming	10	1	--	--
Craft and repair	12	3	12	2
Operatives and				
laborers	9	.3	--	--

Sources: Outlined in appendix A.

Note: Dash (--) indicates there are no hipaygrow occupations in these categories.

attributes, including demographic, attitudinal, and labor market characteristics. Since it is a longitudinal data file, it contains information about the same women from 1968, when the survey began, to 1985, when the latest information is available. Hence, researchers can examine whether the characteristics of women at an early age affect their later labor market choices. It also permits intercohort comparisons, which are discussed in greater detail in the last section of this chapter.

Although NLS data contain a great deal of information about respondents, only women between the ages of 35 to 41 in 1985 are included. Thus, this analysis cannot discuss the characteristics of all women in hipaygrow occupations. Nonetheless, the 35-to-41 age group is of particular interest, since its labor force participation rate is the second highest of all age groups for women, after those between the ages of 18 and 24. Most of these women will have already completed their childbearing. Their current occupation probably represents the type of work they plan to pursue until retirement.

Table 3.4 presents the characteristics of women, aged 35 to 41, who work in hipaygrow occupations. These characteristics are contrasted with the characteristics of other women in the NLS survey. These latter women are divided into two groups: those who work in other jobs that do not fall into hipaygrow occupations and those who do not work in the labor force. To clarify this discussion, female attributes are divided into four groups: educational characteristics, demographic characteristics, attitudinal characteristics, and labor market characteristics. The sample size for this data set is 1,500. Although the NLS contained a total of 3,720 women in its survey as of 1985, this analysis includes only 1,500 women because of the restrictions applied to the sample (discussed in detail in appendix A of this report). There are 288 women in hipaygrow occupations, 725 in other occupations, and 487 not in the paid workforce.

Table 3.4   CHARACERISTICS OF WOMEN AGED 35 TO 41 IN 1985

Characteristics	Women in Hipaygrow Jobs	Women in Other Jobs	Women Not at Work
Educational Charactistics			
Average years completed	14.7	13.0	12.4
Educational Distribution (%)[a]			
Less than four years high school	2	11	20
Four years high school	20	49	46
One to three years college	34	22	17
Four years college	25	9	12
More than four years college	19	9	6
College Major (%)[a]			
Humanities	9	14	16
Education	29	30	36
Business	8	18	12
Social sciences	12	14	11
Natural sciences	2	2	6

Medical sciences	33	8	11
Home economics	2	4	2
Other	6	10	6
Mathematics in High School (%)[a]			
Algebra	92	76	72
Geometry	78	45	43
Trigonometry or calculus	32	13	12
Two years algebra	60	43	45
Educational Goal (%)[a]			
Less than four years high school	1	7	12
Four years high school	20	51	47
Two years college	13	13	12
Four years college	41	16	19
More than four years college	26	13	11
Demographic Characteristics			
Marital Status (%)[a]			
Married	65	65	80
Single	11	7	5
Other	25	27	15

(continued)

Table 3.4   Continued

Characteristics	Women in Hipaygrow Jobs	Women in Other Jobs	Women Not at Work
Demographic Characteristics (*continued*)			
Average number of children	1.6	2.0	2.6
Without children (%)	26	16	10
Black (%)	7	13	12
Geographic Distribution (%)[a]			
In central city	24	27	26
In SMSA outside city	53	43	41
Non-SMSA	23	30	33
Attitudinal Characteristics			
Plans at 35 (%)[a]			
Work	34	32	28
Marry	65	66	70
Other	1	1	2

Is Women's Place at Home? (%)[a]

Agree	23	37	47
Disagree	73	59	48
Don't know	4	5	5

Labor Market Characteristics

Working full-time (%)	81	72	0
Average years of work experience	14	12	6
Average years at home	4	8	15
Hourly pay	$10.98	$7.57	0

Occupational Distribution (%)[a]

Professional	60	15	0
Managerial	25	5	0
Clerical	8	47	0
Sales	5	4	0
Craft	0	2	0
Operatives	0	9	0
Service	3	17	0
Laborers	0	1	0
Sample Size	288	725	487

Source: National Longitudinal Survey of Young Women (for details, see appendix A).
a. Percentages may not add up to 100 because of rounding.

Educational Characteristics

The leading indicator in any labor market analysis is the individual's educational attainment. In this case, education levels differ substantially between those in hipaygrow jobs and those employed in other occupations. On average, women in hipaygrow jobs have 15 years of education; women in other jobs have 13 years. Women who are currently not working have only 12 years of education. More than three-quarters of the women working in hipaygrow jobs have attended college, and about 44 percent completed college, but only about 17 percent of the other women in this age group have completed college. The most popular college major for those in hipaygrow jobs was medical sciences. In fact, one-third of those in hipaygrow jobs who listed a college major reported medical sciences as their college major. Most of these women are working as registered nurses, one of the largest hipaygrow occupations. Only 8 percent of the women working in other jobs listed medical sciences as their college major. In contrast, the most popular college major for these women was education. About 30 percent of those in other occupations who listed a college major reported education as their college major. Most of these women are working as secondary school teachers.

Another major difference in education between each group of women was the number of mathematics courses taken while in high school. Over 90 percent of women in hipaygrow occupations took algebra in high school, and 60 percent took two years of algebra. Almost 80 percent took geometry while in high school and one-third took trigonometry or calculus. On the other hand, women in other jobs and women not at work took fewer mathematics courses while in high school. Less than three-quarters of these women took algebra in high school, and less than half took two years of algebra. Only 43 percent of these women took geometry, compared to nearly 80 percent of women in hipaygrow occupations, and a mere 13 percent took trigonometry or calculus compared to one-third of those in hipaygrow jobs.

Finally, the educational goals of these women when they were between the ages of 18 and 24 differed considerably. Two-thirds of those women who ended up in hipaygrow jobs wanted to complete college; 25 percent wanted to earn advanced degrees. In contrast, only 30 percent of the other women wanted to complete college and only 12 percent wanted to continue beyond college.

Demographic Characteristics

Five basic demographic characteristics are relevant for labor market studies: age, race, marital status, fertility, and geographic location.

AGE AND RACE

Age has already been controlled for by the selection of the sample, which is restricted to those between the ages of 35 and 41. The average age of all three groups of women in table 3.4 is 38. Black women are underrepresented in hipaygrow jobs; they hold only 7 percent of these occupations, yet represent 13 percent of the workforce in other occupations.

MARITAL STATUS AND FERTILITY

The marital status of these women differs as well. Among the women currently working, only 65 percent are married. This percentage does not change for those in hipaygrow jobs compared to those in other paid occupations. In contrast, women in the sample who are not working in the labor force are much more likely to be married (80 percent). Women in hipaygrow jobs are less likely to be divorced and more likely to be single than other working women. Eleven percent of the women in hipaygrow jobs have never been married, while 7 percent of the other working women have remained single. Only 5 percent of the women outside of the workforce have remained single.

Fertility rates among women in hipaygrow jobs are much lower than among women in other jobs or those outside of the workforce. One-fourth of the women in hipaygrow jobs have not had a child. In contrast, 16 percent of the other working women remain childless, and only 10 percent of the women outside of the workforce have had no children. The average number of children for women in hipaygrow jobs is 1.6, for women in other jobs it is 2, and for women outside of the workforce it is 2.6.

GEOGRAPHIC LOCATION

Women who work in hipaygrow occupations are more likely than other women to live in a Standard Metropolitan Statistical Area (SMSA). Three-fourths of the women in hipaygrow occupations live in an SMSA, compared to two-thirds of other women. Moreover, within an SMSA, women in hipaygrow jobs tend to be concentrated outside the central city area. Over half of these women live in an SMSA, but outside a central city. Other women are more evenly distributed; about one-third live outside an SMSA, one-quarter live in a central city, and the remainder live in an SMSA but outside the central city.

Attitudinal Characteristics

This section examines the attitudes of young women toward work and family. The reason for examining women's attitudes at an early stage of life is to determine whether these opinions affect labor market performance later in life. Many economists have argued that women earn less than men because they do not expect to remain in the labor market throughout their adult life. Because of these expectations, it is presumed that women invest less in wage-enhancing human capital than men. Thus, according to this point of view, women do not expect to participate in the labor force continuously, and therefore they invest less in themselves than men, which in turn reduces their relative earnings. This argument implies that a woman's attitude about work and family should influence her labor market outcomes. In particular, it suggests that women who expect to work throughout their adult lives should earn more than other women with similar characteristics. Similarly, these attitudes may encourage a woman to select a hipaygrow job, since such a job offers above-average earnings and employment growth. This attitude was examined using NLS data.

When the respondents were between the ages of 18 and 24 (1968), the NLS asked them: "What would you like to be doing when you are 35 years old?" Most of these women wanted to be out of the labor force at age 35. Only about one-third of the women who were working in 1985, when they were between the ages of 35 and 41, had planned to be working at age 35. Women in hipaygrow jobs were just as likely as other working women to grossly underestimate their future labor force participation. Thus, it does not appear that this particular question had any influence upon the decision to select a hipaygrow job. These questions are discussed in greater detail in appendix A.

When these women were between the ages of 23 and 29 (1973), they were asked whether they agreed with the following statement: "A woman's place is in the home, not in the office or shop." At that time, only 23 percent of the women who selected a hipaygrow job in 1985 agreed with this statement. In contrast, 37 percent of those who selected other jobs in 1985 and 47 percent of those who were out of the workforce in 1985 agreed with this statement. Thus, young women who later selected hipaygrow jobs had quite different attitudes about the general position of women in society than other young women. Although most of these women wanted to be at home with their families at age 35, they didn't agree that a woman's place was necessarily in the home. In contrast, among those women who were at home in 1985, nearly half agreed that a woman's place is in the home when her children are young.

Labor Market Characteristics

A number of different labor market characteristics are examined here, including earnings, hours, occupational distribution, and work experience. The most noteworthy difference between women in hipaygrow jobs and other female workers is the occupational distribution of these two groups. Almost 85 percent of the women working in hipaygrow occupations are employed as professionals and managers. In contrast, two-thirds of the other female workers are employed in clerical occupations, sales, or service work, and only 18 percent work in professional and managerial jobs.

Not surprisingly, the women in hipaygrow occupations earn considerably more than other female workers. In fact, the pay disparity between these groups of female workers exceeds 33 percent. In 1985, women in hipaygrow occupations earned over $10.00 per hour, while other female workers earned $6.61 per hour. The number of hours worked per week also differs slightly. Women who work in hipaygrow jobs work a weekly average of 37.6 hours per week, while women in other jobs work an average of 35.3 hours. Over 75 percent of the women in hipaygrow jobs work full-time, but only two-thirds of the other female workers work full-time.

Finally, women who work in hipaygrow jobs have accumulated an additional 2 years of work experience over women in other jobs. The women in hipaygrow jobs average 14 years of actual work experience at age 38, while other working women average 12 years. Similarly, women in other jobs have spent almost 8 years without working or going to school, but women in hipaygrow jobs have spent only 4 years out of work or school. In contrast, women who are currently out of work have only accumulated 6 years of actual work experience and have spent over 14 years at home.

FACTORS AFFECTING THE DECISION TO ENTER A WELL-PAID, HIGH-GROWTH JOB

This section examines factors that significantly affect a woman's decision to enter a high-paid, high-growth (hipaygrow) occupation. The preceding section reviewed characteristics of women in hipaygrow jobs. This section discusses which, if any, of these factors have a major effect on a woman's occupational choice.

To summarize this section, six factors are found to significantly influence the decision to enter a hipaygrow job. Three of these are related to education, two reflect demographic characteristics, and one pertains to the number of hours worked per week. Women who have majored in science are significantly more likely to work in a hipaygrow job than other women. In addition, women who have taken at least three mathematics courses in high school are more likely to select a hipaygrow occupation than other women. Strong educational goals early in life increase the likelihood that a woman will select a hipaygrow occupation. If a woman works full-time, she is significantly more likely to work in a hipaygrow job than women who work part-time. Women who live in an SMSA but not in the center of the city are more likely to work in hipaygrow occupations. Finally, black women are less likely to work in a hipaygrow job than white women.

Research Method

A bivariate probit model was used to conduct this analysis, the details of which are described in appendix B. The reason for selecting this model over other approaches is that when women enter a hipaygrow job, they actually have made two decisions: first, they have decided to work in the paid labor market; and second, they have decided to select a hipaygrow occupation. Furthermore, these two decisions may be correlated. Neoclassical economic theory suggests that women who work have greater human capital investments than women outside the labor market. In addition, it is assumed that hipaygrow jobs require greater human capital investments than other jobs. Thus, it is hypothesized that these two decisions are positively correlated. In other words, one expects to find that working women tend to choose hipaygrow jobs more often than nonworking women would have if they had decided to work. If these two decisions are correlated, a bivariate probit model will produce consistent parameter estimates for these two decision equations.

Empirical Results

The bivariate probit model was estimated for women using data from the National Longitudinal Survey (NLS) of Young Women. (The characteristics of these data are described in appendix A.) In brief, there are 1,500 women in this sample who range between 35 and 41 years of age. Two-thirds of these women are in the paid workforce. Among those who work, 28 percent are employed in hipaygrow jobs. Table 3.5 defines the variables used in this analysis.

The results of the bivariate probit estimation are presented in table 3.6. Two equations were estimated in this model, each represented by a different column of parameter

Table 3.5 VARIABLE NAMES AND DEFINITIONS

Variable	Definition
Educational Characteristics	
Education	Number of years of schooling completed
Four years of college	1 if went to college at least four years; zero otherwise
Humanities major	1 if college major was in the humanities; zero otherwise
Education major	1 if college major was in education; zero otherwise
Business major	1 if college major was in business; zero otherwise
Social sciences major	1 if college major was in the social sciences; zero otherwise
Home economics major	1 if college major was home economics; zero otherwise
Science major	1 if college major was in the sciences; zero otherwise
Other major	1 if college major was other than those listed above; zero otherwise
Three mathematics courses in high school	1 if took at least three courses in algebra, geometry, trigonometry, or calculus while in high school; zero otherwise

Variable	Definition
Educational goal	Number of years of education a respondent would like to complete (answered at ages 23 to 27)

Demographic Characteristics

Black	1 if black; zero otherwise
Married	1 if married; zero otherwise
Divorced	1 if divorced, widowed, or separated; zero otherwise
Single	1 if single; zero otherwise
Number of children	Number of children under 18 years of age in the home
Children under age three	1 if a child under age three lives in the home; zero otherwise
Children between ages three and five	1 if a child between ages three and five lives in the home; zero otherwise
Children over age five	1 if a child over age five lives in the home; zero otherwise
Central city	1 if live in central city of a Standard Metropolitan Statistical Area (SMSA); zero otherwise
Other SMSA	1 if live in a SMSA but not in the central city; zero otherwise

(continued)

Table 3.5 *Continued*

Variable	Definition
Demographic Characteristics *(continued)*	
South	1 if lives in the South; zero otherwise
Disabled	1 if health limits the amount or kind of work respondent is able to perform; zero otherwise
Other family income	Dollar amount of family income other than respondent's labor income
Age	Age of the individual
Attitudinal Characteristics	
Plan to work at age 35	1 if planned to work at age 35 when respondent was between 18 and 24 years of age; zero otherwise
Negative views on women working	1 if agreed with the statement, "A woman's place is in the home, not in the office or the shop"; zero otherwise
Professional plans	1 if planned to work in a professional or managerial occupation at age 35 when respondent was between 18 and 24 years of age; zero otherwise

Variable	Definition
Labor Market Characteristics	
Work experience	Number of years employed
Home-time	Age minus actual work experience minus education minus 5
Tenure	Number of years worked for current employer
Union contract	1 if wages are set by collective bargaining; zero otherwise
Full-time work	1 if usually work at least 35 hours per week; zero otherwise

Source: National Longitudinal Survey of Young Women, 1985.

estimates in table 3.6. Column two represents the occupation decision and column three the work decision. The results of each decision are discussed here in turn.

The first surprising result is that the estimated correlation between the error terms of these two equations is insignificantly different from zero. In fact, ρ is -.200, with a standard error of .258. As explained earlier, ρ was expected to be positive. Since it is insignificant, this suggests that the two decisions analyzed by this model are independent.

Table 3.6 DETERMINANTS OF WORK AND OCCUPA-
TIONAL DECISION (standard errors in
parentheses)

Variable	Choose Hipaygrow Occupation	Choose to Work
Constant	-2.490** (.726)	-2.359** (.788)
Education	.019 (.051)	.083** (.030)
Four years college	.136 (.224)	
Humanities major	-.290 (.270)	
Education major	.155 (.228)	
Business major	.027 (.233)	
Social sciences major	.289 (.242)	
Home economics major	-.256 (.463)	
Science major	1.110** (.215)	
Other major	.195 (.273)	
Three mathematics courses in high school	.172* (.108)	

Variable	Choose Hipaygrow Occupation	Choose to Work
Educational goal	.094** (.034)	
Married	.122 (.185)	.250 (.217)
Divorced	.197 (.190)	.033 (.208)
Number of children	-.038 (.051)	.043 (.037)
Child over age five		.333** (.168)
Child age five or under		-.410** (.195)
Black	-.307** (.135)	-.156 (.123)
Central city	.013 (.132)	.236** (.117)
Other SMSA	.186* (.118)	.364** (.102)
South		-.135* (.088)
Disabled		-.206 (.118)

(continued)

Table 3.6 *Continued*

Variable	Choose Hipaygrow Occupation	Choose to Work
Other family income		-.2E-04** (.3E-05)
Work experience		.164** (.023)
Home-time	-.024 (.020)	7.8E-04 (.022)
Full-time work	.284** (.133)	
Plan to work at 35	-.028 (.141)	
Negative views on women working	-.074 (.109)	
Professional plans	.161 (.175)	

Source: National Longitudinal Study of Young Women, 1985

Notes: RHO = -.200 (.258); 2 x (log-likelihood) = 2208.6; sample size = 288 for those who choose hipaygrow occupations and 1,500 for those who choose to work.

* Significant at the 15 percent level (two-tailed tests).
** Significant at the 5 percent level (two-tailed tests).

THE OCCUPATIONAL DECISION

The occupational decision is characterized as a dichotomous variable that equals one if the individual selects a hipaygrow occupation, and zero otherwise. A hipaygrow occupation is a job that is both well paid and expected to exhibit above-average growth in the future (see the first section of this chapter for a description of hipaygrow jobs). The independent variables in this equation are of three types: human capital characteristics, demographic characteristics, and attitudinal characteristics. The three corresponding hypotheses in this analysis were: first, that larger human capital investments increase the likelihood that a woman will select a hipaygrow occupation; second, that married women and women with children are less likely to select hipaygrow occupations; and third, that women who had negative attitudes about working outside of the home at an early age will be less likely to select a hipaygrow job.

The results from the occupational selection equation tended to support the first two hypotheses. In terms of investment in human capital, education--especially the type of major a person selects--was found to influence the selection of a hipaygrow occupation. Majoring in science, for example, significantly increases the chance that a woman will enter a hipaygrow job. Majoring in the social sciences also appears to increase the chances that a woman will select a hipaygrow job, while majoring in the humanities appears to decrease those chances. Although these latter coefficients are not significant at the 5 percent level, both are significant at the 30 percent level. This means that there is a 70 percent chance that a woman who majors in one of these areas will behave as described earlier. Although these odds are somewhat lower than generally accepted, the estimated coefficients are larger than the coefficients for the other college majors. Thus, the three college majors with the largest impact on the selection of a hipaygrow occupation are the sciences, the social sciences, and the humanities. Another important factor is whether or not a woman has strong educational goals when she is young. The stronger the educational goals of a young woman, the more likely she is to enter a hipaygrow job later in life. Finally, taking at least three mathematics courses in high school also increases the chances that a woman will select a hipaygrow occupation.

One labor market and two demographic characteristics are important in determining who will select a hipaygrow occupation. First, women who work full-time are significantly more likely to select a hipaygrow job than women who work part-time. Second, being black, rather than white or of another race, significantly reduces the chance that a woman will work in a hipaygrow job. Third, women who live in an SMSA, but not in the central part of a city, are significantly more likely to be employed in a hipaygrow job than women who live in central cities or rural areas.

Finally, although it was hypothesized that a young woman's attitudes about work would influence her choices later in life regarding occupational selection, none of the measures of work attitudes were found to affect a woman's decision to enter a hipaygrow job. Women who wanted to work at age 35 were no more likely to be employed in a hipaygrow job than other women. Furthermore, those women who stated that they would prefer a professional or managerial occupation when they worked at age 35 were no more likely to be in a hipaygrow job than other women. Finally, those women who early in their life believed that a woman's proper place was in the home were slightly less likely to be employed in a hipaygrow job, but this estimated coefficient was insignificant.

THE WORK DECISION

The dependent variable in the first equation is a dichotomous variable that equals one if the woman has paid work, and zero otherwise. The explanatory variables included in this equation are of three types that neoclassical economic theory suggests are pertinent to such an decision: those measuring human capital investments, demographic characteristics, and family income. The corresponding hypotheses were that women with greater amounts of human capital are more likely to be working than women with smaller human capital investments; that married women and women with children are less likely to be working than single women and women without children; and that the presence of other sources of income will reduce the likelihood of women working.

The estimated coefficients for this decision were consistent with these hypotheses. The empirical evidence, for example, showed that women with more education are significantly more likely to work than women with less education. Furthermore, as a woman's work experience increases, so does the likelihood that she will work outside the home. Having other sources of income also decreases the chances that a woman will work.

Other findings were that women with children under the age of six are significantly less likely to work outside the home than other women. Marital status, on the other hand, does not seem to affect the decision to work. Another strong predictor of a woman's decision to work is whether or not she is disabled. Disabled women are significantly less likely to work than able-bodied women. Finally, living in an SMSA significantly increases the likelihood that a woman will work.

INTERCOHORT COMPARISONS

The U.S. Department of Labor has predicted that 40 percent of new jobs created between now and the year 2000 will be in professional, technical, and managerial occupations (Silvestri and Lukasiewicz 1989). The question is: Are young women making the kind of choices today that will allow them to fill these jobs in the future? To answer this question, this section compares the attributes of today's young women (in 1987) with those of women 14 years previously who currently hold hipaygrow jobs. Specifically, the attributes of women between the ages of 23 and 29 in 1987 are compared with those of women who were in this age group 14 years earlier, in 1973. This particular inter-cohort comparison was chosen because it examines the characteristics of women during a critical period in their lives, when major decisions are made about work, education, and family life. This age group spans the years in which most women have finished their formal education and begun their work life. Many also get married and begin having children during this period. An intercohort comparison of this age group determines whether women's choices about these critical issues have changed over time, and whether young women today are making the same kinds of decisions about work, education, and family life that women working in hipaygrow jobs in 1987 made 14 years previously.

In brief, this analysis found that women between the ages of 23 and 29 in 1987 are quite different from the average women in this age group 14 years earlier. On the whole, these changes suggest that young women today are acquiring more human capital and more wage-enhancing human capital than young women before them. However, despite this fact, women from 14 years earlier who now work in hipaygrow occupations exhibited even greater investments in human capital than today's young women. Furthermore, the occupational distribution of this older age group was highly skewed toward professional and managerial occupations when they were 23 to 29, much more so than the occupational distribution of young women today. Thus, this analysis suggests that a higher proportion of young women today may enter hipaygrow jobs than 14 years ago, but that the average young woman today is still unlikely to end up in a hipaygrow job.

The data for this section are derived from the NLS of Youth and the NLS of Young Women. The NLS of Youth contains 4,748 young women and the NLS of Young Women contains 2,167 young women, 344 of whom worked in hipaygrow occupations in 1985. (These data sources and their preparation are described in greater detail in appendix A.)

This section is divided into two parts. The first part is a straightforward intercohort comparison of women between the ages of 23 and 29 in 1973 and 1987. (The characteristics of these young women are reported in the first two columns of table 3.7). The second part is a comparison of the attributes of young women in 1987 with the attributes of young women in 1973 who worked in hipaygrow occupations in 1985. This latter group is a subset of the women in the 1973 sample. The characteristics of this latter group of women are reported in column 4 of table 3.7. All three groups of women average 26 years of age. Their educational, demographic, attitudinal, and labor market characteristics are discussed in the paragraphs following.

An Intercohort Comparison of Women between the Ages of 23 and 29

EDUCATIONAL CHARACTERISTICS

Educational characteristics are the first attributes of young women that are compared in table 3.7. Overall, they show that young women in 1987 have acquired more education and more market-oriented education than young women had in 1973. For example, the average number of years of education that a young woman has completed has increased to 13 years, up from 12.7 in 1973. Although this increase appears slight, it is significant and masks a major change within the distribution of education. Today's young women are much more likely to attend or complete college than young women before them. In 1987, 44 percent of young women had gone to college, up from 37 percent in 1973. The high school dropout rate had also declined sharply. In 1973, 17 percent of the women in this age group had not completed high school, but this rate had dropped to 11 percent by 1987.

The distribution of college majors among young women has changed dramatically since 1973. In 1973, over 50 percent of the women listing a college major indicated that either education or medical sciences was their college major. By 1987, these two majors had fallen to 30 percent of all college majors. Meanwhile, business had become the most popular major among young women, capturing 28 percent of all college majors.

The number of mathematics courses that young women take while in high school has seriously declined, according to NLS data, leaving one area of educational preparation sorely lacking among young women today. In 1987, only 63 percent of young women in their mid-twenties had taken algebra while in high school, and less than a quarter had taken two years of algebra. Only 38 percent enrolled in high school geometry, and a mere 6 percent attempted trigonometry or calculus at the high school level. These figures contrast sharply with the levels of mathematics taken in high school by women who graduated from high school in the mid-1960s. Almost 80 percent of these women took algebra in high school and nearly 50 percent took two years of this subject. Over half of these women took geometry and 17 percent attempted trigonometry or calculus while in high school.

It should be noted, however, that the NLS uses different methods of collecting data on high school mathematics

Table 3.7 INTERCOHORT COMPARISON OF WOMEN AGED 23-29 IN 1973 AND 1987

Characteristics	Women 23-29 in 1987	Women 23-29 in 1973	Women 23-29 in 1973 but Work in Hipaygrow in Hipaygrow Jobs in 1985
Educational Characteristics			
Average years completed	13	12.7	14
Educational Distribution (%)[a]			
Less than four years high school	11	17	4
Four years high school	46	45	29
One to three years college	23	20	34
Four years college	16	14	26
More than four years college	5	4	7
College Major (%)[a]			
Humanities	10	17	13
Education	15	33	30
Business	28	6	4
Social sciences	8	13	13

Natural sciences	4	5	3
Medical sciences	16	18	30
Home economics	2	3	3
Other	18	5	5
Mathematics in High School (%)[a]			
Algebra	63	79	92
Geometry	38	52	78
Trigonometry or calculus	6	17	31
Two years algebra	23	48	58
Educational Goal (%)[a]			
Less than four years high school	2	7	1
Four years high school	32	42	20
Two years college	18	12	13
Four years college	31	22	41
More than four years college	17	16	25
Demographic Characteristics			
Marital Status (%)[a]			
Married	53	76	71
Single	34	14	20

(continued)

Table 3.7   Continued

Characteristics	Women 23-29 in 1987	Women 23-29 in 1973	Women 23-29 in 1973 but Work in Hipaygrow Jobs in 1985
Marital Status (*continued*)			
Other	14	9	9
Without children (%)	47	34	46
Average age	26	26	26
Attitudinal Characteristics			
Plans at 35 (%)[a]			
Work	67	32	35
Marry	27	66	64
Other	6	2	1
Is Women's Place at Home? (%)[a]			
Agree	9	59	73
Disagree	90	37	22
Don't know	1	5	5

Labor Market Characteristics

Working (%)	67	53	72
Working full-time (%)	74	74	79
Average years of work experience	3.9	3.2	4
Occupational Distribution (%)[a]			
Professional	10	3	4
Managerial	20	22	45
Clerical	33	37	32
Sales	6	5	2
Craft	2	1	1
Operatives	6	13	5
Private household	4	4	2
Service	16	15	9
Farm	0	1	0
Laborers	1	0	0
Sample Size	4,748	2,167	344

Sources: National Longitudinal Surveys of Young Women and Youth (for details, see appendix A).

a. Percentages may not add up to 100 because of rounding.

courses. The NLS of Youth has painstakingly added high school transcript information to the original survey data. Thus, for the young women in 1987, their mathematics information is collected from their actual high school transcripts. The NLS of Young Women, on the other hand, asks the respondents to recall how many mathematics courses they took while in high school. Thus, the number of such courses taken by young women in 1973 is based upon a respondent's memory rather than actual transcript information.

Although this difference in data sources may explain part of the large difference in high school mathematics courses taken between 1973 and 1987, it probably does not explain all of it. Another compelling explanation is that young women in 1987 had considerably more elective courses to choose from while attending high school than young women in 1973. These young women graduated from high school between 1976 and 1982, during a time when high school curricula had been expanded. Many young women may have taken advantage of this expansion and decided not to take second- and third-year mathematics courses. In contrast, young women in 1973 graduated from high school between 1961 and 1967. During this period, course selection was quite limited, and young people might have taken mathematics courses because they had such limited choice. On the other hand, some of these new elective courses include training in mathematics, such as economics, statistics, and computer science. Hence, a comparison between the number of mathematics courses taken by young women in high school around 1980 and the number taken by young women 14 years earlier may be misleading.

The NLS asked both sets of young women: "How much education would you like to get?" This question was asked of the young women in 1968 and 1982, when they were between the ages of 18 and 24. This report's analysis found that young women who reached their 20s in the 1980s had much higher educational goals than the young women who reached their 20s in the late 1960s. Two-thirds of the young women in 1982 wanted to attend college, and almost half wanted to complete college. In contrast, about half of the young women in 1968 wanted to attend college, and 38 percent wanted to complete college.

DEMOGRAPHIC CHARACTERISTICS

The demographic changes among this cohort of women have already been noted by many authors. It is well known that women in their 20s are much more likely to be single and childless today than women before them. In 1987, one-third of the young women were single and just over half were married. Fourteen years earlier, over 75 percent of women in this age cohort were married and only 14 percent remained single. Almost half of the young women in 1987 were childless; two-thirds of the women in 1973 had children.

ATTITUDINAL CHARACTERISTICS

Of the numerous attitudinal questions asked by the NLS, two are examined here. Both questions ask women about their views regarding the trade-off between work and family. First, the NLS asks: "What would you like to be doing when you are 35 years old?" The women could answer: (1) working, (2) married, having a family, or (3) other. Second, the NLS asks women whether they agree or disagree with the following statement: "A woman's place is in the home, not in the office or shop." Thus, the first question asks for a personal assessment of the choice between work and family, and the second asks about a woman's general attitude on this issue.

Not surprisingly, the attitudes of young women toward work have changed considerably. Over 90 percent of the young women surveyed in 1987 disagreed that a woman's proper place was in the home. Just 14 years earlier, about a third disagreed with this statement. Similarly, their plans for their own lives have changed. Now two-thirds of young women in their 20s want to work at age 35. Fourteen years ago, two-thirds of the women in this age group wanted to be married and raising a family.

LABOR MARKET CHARACTERISTICS

It is well known that the proportion of women in their mid-20s who are working has steadily increased over time. By 1987, two-thirds of women between the ages of 23 and 29 were working, up from just over half in 1973. About three-fourths of the women who are employed work full-time. This is the same proportion as in 1973. On the other hand, young women's actual work experience has increased, from 3.2 years in 1973 to 3.9 years in 1987.

The occupational distribution of young women has also changed during this period. Young women today are much more likely to work in managerial occupations than their predecessors. In 1987, 10 percent of the women between the ages of 23 and 29 worked as managers, up from 3 percent in 1973. On the other hand, the chances that a woman works as an operative has significantly declined. Only 6 percent of these women work as operatives in 1987, down from 13 percent in 1973. Although one-third of these young women still work as clericals, this is a significant decline from 1973 when 37 percent of the young women worked in this occupation. Finally, the proportion of women working in services has significantly increased from 1973 to 1987.

Intercohort Comparison of Young Women in 1987 and Young Women in 1973 Who Later Chose a Hipaygrow Occupation

EDUCATIONAL CHARACTERISTICS

Young women from 1973 who selected hipaygrow jobs later in life had significantly higher levels of education but more traditionally female college majors than young women from the same age group in 1987. Young women who ended up in hipaygrow jobs had an average of 14 years of education in 1973; young women in 1987 had only 13 years. Furthermore, two-thirds of these older women had attended college in 1973; less than 50 percent of the young women in 1987 had attended college. Although the older women had significantly more education, they selected college majors that were quite traditional for women; over 60 percent of these women had majored in education or medical sciences. In contrast, only 30 percent of the young women in 1987 majored in these fields. As mentioned earlier, the largest college major for young women today is business. Almost 30 percent of young women between 23 and 29 years of age in 1987 had chosen this major.

In 1973, young women who later worked in a hipaygrow job had taken significantly more mathematics courses while in high school than young women in 1987. Over 90 percent of these older women took algebra in high school, and almost 60 percent took two years of this subject. Almost 80 percent took high school geometry and 30 percent took trigonometry or calculus. In contrast, most young women today have taken only one college preparatory mathematics course.

Finally, young women in 1973 who later selected hipaygrow jobs had significantly higher educational goals when they were young than young women have today. Nearly 80 percent of these older women said they wanted to attend college; two-thirds said they wanted to complete college. In contrast, most of today's young women say they would like to attend college, but less than half say they would like to complete college. Clearly, the young women in 1973 who later ended up in hipaygrow jobs were highly motivated and well-educated, more so than the average young woman today.

DEMOGRAPHIC AND ATTITUDINAL CHARACTERISTICS

The marital status of the young women in 1973 who later worked in hipaygrow jobs is quite different from young women in 1987. In fact, it is more like that of the average young woman in 1973. For instance, over 70 percent of these older women were married in 1973, whereas about half of the young women in 1987 were married. One-fifth of the young women in 1973 who ended up in hipaygrow jobs were single; one-third of the young women in 1987 remain single.

In contrast, the fertility status of these two groups of women is quite similar. Forty-six percent of the women in 1973 who later worked in hipaygrow jobs remained childless; 47 percent of the women in 1987 had no children. In contrast, two-thirds of the entire population of women between 23 and 29 in 1973 had children.

The attitudinal characteristics of the group of women in 1973 who later chose hipaygrow jobs are quite surprising. Although all of these women were working in 1985 when they were between the ages of 35 and 41, only one-third said at an early age (between 18 and 24) that they wanted to work at age 35. Similarly, at this same early age, over 70 percent of these women agreed that a woman's place was in the home, not on the job. Yet, all of these women ended up working outside the home. In contrast, two-thirds of the young women in 1987 said they wanted to work at age 35, and only 10 percent agreed that a woman's place is in the home.

LABOR MARKET CHARACTERISTICS

The young women in 1973 who later worked in hipaygrow jobs established a different labor market role for themselves than the one selected by young women from the same age group in 1987. For instance, the former are more likely to be working than the latter. In addition, a larger proportion of these women work full-time compared to young women in 1987. But most importantly, they have already selected a significantly different set of occupations than young women in 1987. Almost half of these women already worked as professionals or managers when they were between the ages of 23 and 29. In contrast, in 1987 only 30 percent of women in this age group worked in these occupations.

Notes, chapter 3

1. Appendix A explains how these jobs were identified.

2. This section relies heavily on Silvestri and Lukasiewicz (1989).

3. The skill requirements of hipaygrow jobs were examined using information from the fourth edition of the *Dictionary of Occupational Titles*. This publication quantifies numerous attributes of jobs, including their general education (GED) and specific training (SVP) requirements. Miller et al. (1980) review this information for the 500 or so occupations included in the Standard Occupational Classification (SOC) system. Neither the GED nor SVP figures are measured in years, but this analysis translated them into years using the *Handbook for Analyzing Jobs* (U.S. Department of Labor 1972).

4

ECONOMIC CHARACTERISTICS OF CONTINUOUS AND INTERMITTENT FEMALE WORKERS

Many economists have maintained that women earn less than men because they are less committed to the workforce than men (Fuchs 1988; Smith and Ward 1984). In essence, it is argued that women, on average, feel a stronger desire for children than men do and a greater concern for their children's welfare after they are born. This desire and concern cause women to focus upon their role as mother and deemphasize their work life. Examples are cited regularly to demonstrate that women deemphasize their work life compared to men. It is argued, for instance, that most young women are less likely than men to invest in wage-enhancing human capital while in school. This is reflected in their choice of major and their reluctance to enter advanced degree programs in business, medicine, and law. In addition, women are presumably more likely to accept lower wages in exchange for shorter and more flexible hours, a job location near home, and limited out-of-town travel so that they can meet the demands of their families.

Perhaps the most important example often cited to demonstrate the ways in which women deemphasize their work life is that women tend to leave the labor market for extended periods of time during childbirth and when their children are young. These interruptions reduce women's future earnings because their skills depreciate during their time out of the labor force. Furthermore, they are not acquiring the training and work experience that lead to higher earnings in the future. On the other hand, men remain in the labor market throughout their adult life, gaining the necessary human capital to enhance their earnings. This difference between female and male labor force participation is typically pointed to as the most glaring example of how women are less committed to the workforce than men and thus earn less than men (Mincer and Polachek 1974).

A number of studies have attempted to estimate the extent to which intermittent labor force participation reduces women's earnings relative to those of men. Mincer and Polachek (1974), who were among the first to study this issue, found that 35 percent of the male-female earnings gap could be attributed to differences in work experience and time at home. A more recent study has predicted that as much as 90 percent of the earnings disparity between women and men can be explained by differences in accumulated human capital (Goldin and Polachek 1987). Still others argue that intermittent work behavior explains little of the pay disparity between women and men (Duncan and Gregory 1979). A recent U.S. Bureau of the Census (1987) report found that about 20 percent of the earnings gap was due to differences in work experience.

Yet, empirical research has not compared the labor market outcomes of women who work continuously to those of women who work intermittently. An examination of these outcomes could determine the extent to which continuous work behavior contributes to the male-female pay differential. If women who work continuously experience significantly different labor market outcomes from other women, this result suggests that intermittent labor force behavior is a principal factor leading to the male-female pay disparity. On the other hand, if women who work continuously experience similar labor market outcomes as other women, this result suggests that intermittence is not a major factor contributing to the pay disparity between women and men.

Previous research on this topic has compared the earnings of men who tend to work continuously with the earnings of women who generally work intermittently. But this pay differential may be influenced by discrimination as well as the decision whether or not to work continuously. The benefit of this approach is that it isolates the economic gain from working continuously from other factors that influence the male-female earnings differential, such as discrimination.

RESEARCH METHOD

The standard method for analyzing the pay disparity between women and men is first to estimate separate earnings equations for women and men. The mean pay difference between the sexes is then decomposed into two parts: (1) that which is due to mean differences in productivity-related characteristics and (2) that which is due to differences in estimated coefficients (Blinder 1973; Oaxaca 1973). This latter component is then referred to as the *unexplained portion* of the analysis, since it is unexplained by factors in the analysis.

This approach has been recently expanded to take into account selectivity bias that may result from an individual's decision about whether or not to work. Gronau (1974) and others have argued that when examining employer treatment of two groups, the research should focus on wage offers rather than observed wages. Since the latter are influenced by individuals' decisions about whether or not to accept paid work, analyses of observed wages may yield biased estimates of mean wage offers to individuals as well as biased estimated coefficients in the earnings equation. The direction of this bias may be either positive or negative. If the wage regression tends to include those with higher wage offers, then the bias will be positive. In other words, the mean of observed wages will be higher than the mean wage offer. On the other hand, if inclusion in the sample is selective of those with low wage offers, then the bias will be negative; that is, the mean of observed wages will be higher than the mean wage offer.

The technique suggested by Heckman (1979) to correct for this selectivity bias is to include the inverse of Mills' ratio as an explanatory variable in the wage regression. The inverse of Mills' ratio is obtained from a probit equation that predicts whether or not an individual decides to work for pay. Thus, the implicit decision of whether or not to work is explicitly modeled and taken into account when estimating the wage equation.

This same method could be used to analyze the pay difference between women who work continuously and women who work intermittently. Separate earnings equations could be estimated for women who work continuously and women who work intermittently after correcting for possible selectivity bias due to the work decision. But another source of possible selectivity bias still exists. Whether or not a woman decides to work continuously or intermittently is also an underlying decision that a woman makes. If this decision is correlated with the error term in the earnings equation, a standard Heckman-selection estimated wage equation will yield inconsistent parameter estimates. This decision and the wage equation error term are most likely correlated, since the unmeasured characteristics that enhance earnings, such as self-motivation and intelligence, are also likely to influence a woman's decision to work continuously. Neoclassical economic theory suggests that the decision to work continuously will depend, in part, upon a woman's stock of human capital, her marital and fertility status, and her attitudes toward work. Yet, these are precisely the type of factors that are expected to influence earnings. Any unmeasured aspect of these characteristics will influence both the individual's earnings and her decision to work continuously. Thus, it is anticipated that the error term in the earnings equations will be correlated with the decision whether or not to work continuously. Consequently, this section estimates a model that corrects for both sources of possible selectivity bias: labor market participation and the decision about whether or not to work continuously. Appendix B formulates this bivariate probit selection model.

EMPIRICAL RESULTS

The bivariate selectivity model has four equations to be estimated. The first equation examines the factors influencing the decision about whether or not to work continuously. The second analyzes the determinants of the work decision. Separate earnings equations are then estimated for continuous and intermittent workers. They are first estimated using ordinary least squares (OLS) regression analysis. Then they are reestimated once the two selection-correction variables generated from the bivariate probit analysis are included in the earnings equations. Before presenting the results of this model, however, descriptive characteristics of the women who work continuously and intermittently are reviewed.

Descriptive Characteristics

This analysis uses data from the National Longitudinal Survey (NLS) of Young Women. (A longer description of this data and its preparation are given in appendix A.) Table 4.1 presents the average characteristics of women who were between the ages of 35 and 41 in 1985. The columns correspond to three different cells from the double

Table 4.1   CHARACTERISTICS OF WOMEN AGED 35 TO 41 IN 1985

Characteristics	Women Who Are at Work and Have Worked Continuously	Women Who Are at Work but Have Not Worked Continuously	Women Who Are Not at Work and Have Not Worked Continuously
Educational Characteristics			
Average years completed	16.0	13.1	12.4
Educational Distribution (%)[a]			
Less than four years high school	0	10	21
Four years high school	5	46	46
One to three years college	29	25	17
Four years college	25	12	11
More than four years college	41	7	5
Demographic Characteristics			
Average age	36	38	38
Without children (%)	49	14	9

Marital Status (%)[a]			
Married	57	67	80
Single	23	6	5
Other	20	27	15
Attitudinal Characteristics (%)[a]			
Plan to work at age 35	31	33	28
Agree that woman's place is in the home	17	35	47
Labor Market Characteristics			
Hourly pay	$10.58	$7.08	--
Average years of work experience	16.4	12.0	5.9
Average years at home	0	7.9	14.6
Sample Size	146	867	481

Source: National Longitudinal Survey of Young Women, 1985.

a. Percentages may not add up to 100 because of rounding.

selection rule described above: those women who work both continuously and currently; those who choose not to work continuously, but are currently working; and those who decided not to work continuously or currently. The fourth group of women, those who decided to work continuously but not currently, had only six individuals. Hence, their characteristics are not reported here.

There are a total of 1,500 women in the sample, two-thirds of whom are working. Among those who are working, 86 percent have worked intermittently and 12 percent have worked continuously. Thus, in this age group, women who have decided to work continuously and are currently employed represent a small minority of women. Their demographic characteristics are also quite different from other working women. They have acquired considerably more education, averaging 16 years, compared to 13 years for other working women. They are also much more likely to have remained single and childless. About one-fourth of these women have never married. Among other working women, only 6 percent remain single. Half of the women who work continuously have never had children; 14 percent of other working women remain childless, and only 9 percent of nonworking women have had no children. Women who have worked continuously also have acquired much more work experience than other women, even though the former tend to be about two years younger. Women who work continuously in this sample average 36 years of age and have over 16 years of work experience. In contrast, other working women are about 38 years old and have about 12 years of work experience. Finally, the women in the first group earn considerably more per hour than other working women. In 1985, they earned $10 per hour; other working women earned $7 per hour.

It is important to note, however, that although the characteristics of women who work continuously are quite different from those of other working women, they are also quite different from those of the average male worker. According to data from the Panel Study of Income Dynamics (PSID), the average 36-year-old male worker has 14 years of education and 17 years of work experience compared to the 16 years of each that continuous female workers have. Furthermore, they are more likely to be married with children than the average continuous female worker. Eighty-two percent of the 36-year-old male workers were married, and three-fourths had children. Among the continuous female workers, 57 percent were married and one-half had children.

Bivariate Probit Model Results

The bivariate selectivity model has four equations that need to be estimated. The first two equations are the two decision rules: whether or not to work and whether or not to work continuously. These two equations were estimated using a bivariate probit model. The last two equations are the earnings equations, the results of which are discussed in the next section.

The first equation in the bivariate probit model estimates the decision about whether or not to work continuously. This decision is characterized as a dichotomous variable that equals one if the women decides to work continuously, and zero otherwise. The explanatory variables include human capital, demographic, and attitudinal characteristics (their precise definitions are given in table 3.5). It was anticipated that women with greater investments in human capital would be more likely to work continuously. It was also hypothesized that women who work continuously would more likely be single and childless. Finally, it was hypothesized that women with positive attitudes toward working would be more likely to work continuously than women with negative attitudes about this issue.

The second equation in the bivariate probit model describes the work decision, which is characterized as a dichotomous variable that equals one if the women is working, and zero otherwise. The explanatory variables included in this equation are of three types suggested by neoclassical theory: those measuring human capital investments, demographic characteristics, and family income. It was hypothesized that women with greater amounts of human capital are more likely to be working than women with smaller human capital investments; further, that married women and women with children are less likely to be working than single women and women without children; and, finally, that the presence of other sources of income will reduce the likelihood of women working.

The bivariate probit results are presented in table 4.2. The first noteworthy result is the estimated correlation between the error terms of these two equations, or ρ, which is .263 with a standard error of .124. This means that, as expected, the error terms in these two equations are significantly positively correlated. Presumably, women who decide to work in a particular year are more likely to have worked continuously in the past than women who decide not to work. The characteristics that encourage women to

Table 4.2 DETERMINANTS OF WORK DECISION AND
DECISION TO WORK CONTINUOUSLY
(standard errors in parentheses)

Variable	Decision to Work Continuously	Decison to Work Currently
Constant	7.414 ** (1.673)	-2.052 ** (.794)
Education	.389 ** (.047)	.080 ** (.030)
Married		.219 (.218)
Divorced		.017 (.207)
Single	.476 ** (.204)	
Number of children	-.210 ** (.067)	.037 (.038)
Children under age three	-.204 (.260)	-.389 ** (.200)
Children between ages three and five	-.026 (.284)	-.263 (.215)
Children over age five	-.385 ** (.192)	.330 ** (.171)
Black	-.012 (.158)	-.169 (.123)
Central city		.244 ** (.117)

Variable	Decision to Work Continuously	Decison to Work Currently
Other SMSA		.351 ** (.102)
South		-.115 (.088)
Disabled		-.193 * (.117)
Home-time		-.009 (.022)
Other family income		-.2E-04 (.3E-05)
Work experience		.151 ** (.024)
Age	-.355 ** (.051)	
Plan to work at age 35	-.003 (.130)	
Negative views on women working	-.100 (.157)	
Educational goal	-.042 (.049)	

Source: National Longitudinal Survey of Young Women (1985).

Notes, table 4.2

See table 3.5 for definitions of these variables. RHO = .263**
(.124); -2* (log-likelihood) = 1776.8; sample size = 1,500.

* Significant at the 15 percent level (two-tailed tests).
** Significant at the 5 percent level (two-tailed tests).

work in a particular year are similar, indeed identical in many instances, to the characteristics that encourage women to work continuously. Thus, I had expected to find a positive correlation between these two error terms.

Overall, the results from the decision about whether or not to work continuously tended to support the previously stated hypotheses. For example, large investments in education increase the likelihood that a woman will work continuously. Also, women who never marry and remain childless are significantly more likely to work continuously than other women. In addition, more children increase the chances that a woman will not work continuously. On the other hand, variables measuring a woman's attitudes about work had no impact on the decision to work continuously.

The estimated coefficients for the determinants of the work decision were also consistent with neoclassical theory. The empirical evidence, for example, supported the hypothesis that larger human capital investments increase the likelihood that a woman will decide to work. Furthermore, women with children under three years of age are significantly less likely to work than women with older children or no children. Having other sources of income also decreases the chances that a woman will work.

Results from the Earnings Equations

The third and fourth equations of the bivariate selectivity model are the earnings equations for women who work continuously and women who work intermittently. These two equations were first estimated using ordinary least-squares regression analysis. These estimations, however, yielded inconsistent population parameters, since the subsamples used in each regression were not randomly selected. Consequently, the earnings equations were reestimated once the two selectivity-correction variables generated from the bivariate probit model were included in the analysis.

The explanatory variables included in this analysis are standard regressors. Human capital characteristics were measured by education, actual work experience, and employer tenure. Demographic characteristics included race, marital status, and fertility. Three geographic factors were also included--whether an individual lives in the South, in a central city, or in a Standard Metropolitan Statistical Area (SMSA) but not in the central city. Finally, union status was also included as an explanatory variable. A dummy variable was included that equals one if a woman is covered by a collective bargaining unit, and zero otherwise.

Table 4.3 reports the results of the estimated earnings equations, first without the selection-correction variables and then with these variables. The selectivity results are worth reviewing first, since they distinguish the two estimations. The first selectivity variable measured the possible selectivity bias from the work decision. This estimated coefficient was significantly positive in both of

Table 4.3 LOG EARNINGS REGRESSION RESULTS WITH AND WITHOUT SELECTIVITY BIAS CORRECTION (standard errors in parentheses)

Variable	Results without Bias Correction		Results with Bias Correction	
	Continuous Workers	Intermittent Workers	Continuous Workers	Intermittent Workers
Constant	2.104** (.654)	.476** (.113)	1.389* (.971)	-.003 (.241)
Education	.014 (.022)	.071** (.007)	.051 (.043)	.072** (.010)
Work experience	-.024 (.025)	.032** (.004)	-.031 (.033)	.056** (.010)
Employer tenure	.001** (.001)	.001** (.2E-03)	.001** (5.1E-04)	.001** (2.5E-04)
Single	.036 (.085)	-.105** (.060)	.071 (.115)	-.137** (.068)

No. of children	-.012 (.030)	-.012 (.012)	-.064 (.067)	4.5E-04 (.014)
Children under three	-.181* (.116)	.211** (.079)	-.255 (.183)	.056 (.111)
Black	-.038 (.097)	-.146** (.039)	-.069 (.135)	-.158** (.044)
Central city	.362** (.094)	.178** (.039)	.400** (.096)	.203** (.047)
Other SMSA	.427** (.083)	.196** (.035)	.441** (.083)	.225** (.042)
South	-.069 (.076)	-.096** (.031)	-.082 (.074)	-.117** (.037)
Union contract	-.022 (.072)	.081** (.035)	-.023 (.072)	.084** (.035)
lambda-1			.679* (.422)	
lambda-2			.259* (.181)	

(continued)

Table 4.3 *Continued*

Variable	Results without Bias Correction		Results with Bias Correction	
	Continuous Workers	Intermittent Workers	Continuous Workers	Intermittent Workers
lambda-3				.336**
				(.132)
lambda-4				-.116*
				(.062)
Adjusted R^2	.14	.35	.16	.36
Sample Size	146	867	146	867

Source: National Longitudinal Survey of Young Women (1985).

Notes: See table 3.5 for definitions of these variables.

* Significant at the 15 percent level (two-tailed tests).
** Significant at the 5 percent level (two-tailed tests).

the earnings equations that correct for selectivity. This means that working women have higher wage offers than nonworking women with similar measured characteristics, suggesting that working women have greater wage-enhancing unmeasured characteristics than nonworking women.

The second selectivity variable measured the possible selectivity bias due to the decision about whether or not to work continuously. This analysis expected to find positive selection. In other words, it was anticipated that women who worked continuously would have higher earnings than other women with similar characteristics if they had decided to work continuously. The same applies for women who decide to work intermittently; I expected to find that their earnings were higher than other women with similar characteristics had they decided to work intermittently. Since the value of this variable is positive for women who work continuously and negative for women who work intermittently, positive selectivity would exist if the coefficient for the selectivity variable is positive for women who work continuously and negative for women who work intermittently. Consistent evidence was found to support the hypothesis of positive selectivity. Both estimated coefficients have the anticipated signs and are significant at the 15 percent level.

Table 4.3 also shows that the adjusted R^2 is much larger in the intermittent workers equation than in the continuous worker equation. Furthermore, it increases slightly for both types of workers when the selectivity variables are added to the analysis. This suggests that conventional factors generally included in earnings equations explain more of the wage variation among intermittent female workers than among continuous female workers. In addition, it suggests that correcting for selectivity biases increases the explanatory power of these earnings equations for both types of workers.

A number of surprising results are also presented in table 4.3. In particular, some of the estimated coefficients for the equations that correct for selectivity bias were not as expected. For example, among intermittent female workers, single women earn significantly less than married or divorced women. On the other hand, marital status has no significant impact on earnings for those women who work continuously. I had expected to find that single women earned significantly more than other women, regardless of whether they had worked intermittently or continuously. A second example occurs among the variables that measure the extent of childbearing. Having children was not found to significantly reduce the earnings of either continuous or intermittent female workers. Finally, although all three measures of human capital investment had significantly positive estimated coefficients for intermittent workers, only one of these--employer tenure--was significantly positive for continuous female workers. The estimated coefficients for education and actual work experience were insignificant for these women.

Estimated Pay Differentials

The mean value of the logarithmic wage for women who work continuously is 2.335; for women who work intermittently it is 1.928. Thus, the difference between the mean values is .407. This means that the average pay of female workers who work intermittently would have to increase 50 percent to equal that earned by women who work continuously.[1] This pay differential is sizable and is similar in magnitude to the gross pay differential between women and men. It suggests that a large portion of the pay differential between women and men is due to their different attachments to the labor force. However, as is shown here, this gross differential is somewhat misleading.

As explained earlier, the pay differential may be divided into two parts: that which is explained by differences in explanatory variables and that which is explained by differences in estimated coefficients. This latter term is estimated in this section and is referred to as the *unexplained pay disparity* between continuous and intermittent female workers. These estimates were first calculated using estimated coefficients from the earnings equations that have corrected for selectivity bias. Using notation previously introduced, the estimated pay differential between continuous and intermittent female workers is:

$$g_A = (B_2 - B_1)' \overline{X}_1 +$$

$$(a_3 - a_1) \overline{\lambda} + (a_4 - a_2) \overline{\lambda}_2, \tag{4.1}$$

where: the subscript A indicates that this estimate was adjusted for possible selectivity bias. In other words, the pay differential is equal to the difference in the estimated coefficients in the two wage equations, weighted by the mean value of the explanatory variables for intermittent female workers. The corresponding percentage pay differential is:

$$G_A = e^{g_A} - 1. \qquad (4.2)$$

To interpret this result, consider the following conceptual experiment. From a sample of women who have decided to work intermittently, pick at random an individual with the average characteristics of women in this category. Then predict a logarithmic wage for this individual if she worked intermittently and continuously. The percentage difference between these two wages is then equal to G_A. That is, G_A is based upon a conditional experiment where women have already opted for intermittent employment.[2]

In this case, G_A is equal to .169, meaning that women who work intermittently earn about 17 percent less than they would if they had decided to work continuously. Furthermore, 62 percent of the gross pay differential is explained by mean differences in characteristics between these two types of workers; 38 percent remains unexplained by the characteristics included in this analysis.[3]

This pay differential can also be estimated using coefficients from an ordinary least-squares analysis of the earnings equations. In this case,

$$g_U = (C_2 - C_1)'\overline{X}_1, \qquad (4.3)$$

where the subscript U indicates that this estimate was not adjusted for possible selectivity bias and the Cs are the estimated coefficients from the ordinary least-squares analysis. The corresponding percentage differential is then:

$$G_U = e^{g_U} - 1. \tag{4.4}$$

In this case, G_U is equal to .453, suggesting that intermittent female workers earn about 45 percent less than they would if they had decided to work continuously. Clearly, estimating separate earnings equations for intermittent and continuous female workers without correcting for selectivity biases overestimates the unexplained portion of the pay differential between these two groups of female workers. G_A, in contrast, shows that a great deal of the pay gap between intermittent and continuous female workers is due to differences in their characteristics, leaving 38 percent of the total pay gap unexplained.

To summarize, these results show that women who work continuously earn 50 percent more than women who work intermittently. Furthermore, most of this pay differential is due to differences in measured characteristics, such as education and work experience, and not differences in estimated coefficients. The mean difference in education, for example, explains almost 40 percent of the total pay differential between these two groups of women. Women do gain a wage premium, however, if they work continuously. It is estimated that the hourly pay of a woman who works intermittently would increase by 17 percent if she worked continuously. This wage premium explains 38 percent of the total pay differential between continuous and intermittent female workers. The remaining 62 percent of the pay gap is due to mean differences in explanatory variables. Hence, women who work continuously experience better labor market outcomes than other female workers after productivity characteristics are taken into account, but most of their higher pay is due to productivity differences. This suggests that a factor contributing to the pay disparity between men and women is that the average male works continuously whereas the average female does not, but this factor alone does not explain the majority of the male-female pay differential.

Notes, chapter 4

1. $.502 = e^{.407} - 1.$

2. It is also possible to estimate this pay differential without including the selectivity variables. In other words,

$$g_A = (B_2 - B_1)' \overline{X}_1.$$

This definition corresponds to a different conceptual experiment, which seemed less appropriate for these purposes. In such a case, the conceptual experiment selects any woman with the average characteristics of intermittent female workers. Then a logarithmic wage is predicted for this woman if she were employed in a female-dominated job and a non-female-dominated job. In other words, this definition is based upon an unconditional experiment in which the underlying decision processes are modeled in addition to specifying the earnings structures for the two types of workers. For a more complete discussion of these various definitions, see Duncan and Leigh (1980).

3. $.38 = g_A / .407,$

where .407 is the gross pay differential.

5

CONCLUSIONS

The gender gap in earnings decreased dramatically in the 1980s, in sharp contrast to the previous two decades when the pay ratio between women and men hovered around 59 percent. Although different measures of earnings and different data sources can be used to examine this issue, all show a consistent pattern of rising earnings for women relative to men during the 1980s. However, despite this dramatic increase, surprisingly little empirical research has examined why it occurred.

Five explanations have been given for why the male-female pay disparity narrowed during the 1980s. They are:

1. The skills of female workers improved relative to male workers, contributing to the rise in women's relative pay.

2. Labor market discrimination against women declined.

3. The industrial distribution of employment shifted in the 1980s away from unionized, energy-intensive, and foreign-trade sensitive industries, owing, in part, to the oil shock of 1979, the back-to-back recessions in 1980-82, and the overvaluation of the dollar in the 1980s. This industrial restructuring of the economy may have negatively affected male workers more than female workers, thus contributing to the rise in women's relative pay.

4. The wage premiums previously available to male workers in certain sectors of the economy, such as unionized firms, have declined during the 1980s for the same reasons described in explanation number three. These changes may have contributed to the narrowing of the sex pay differential.

5. The occupational distribution of male and female workers may have converged over time, contributing to the increase in the relative pay of women.

Although previous research has examined some of these explanations, their relative merits have not been fully explored. Hence, the research reported here evaluates the relative merits of these explanations. It found that among a number of factors contributing to the rise in women's relative pay, the most salient factor was the change in the occupational characteristics of male and female workers. Other factors included: (1) a decline in labor market discrimination against women; (2) a rise in the relative quality of female labor; and (3) a convergence in the industrial distribution of male and female workers. Since all of these factors are likely to continue to change in a manner favorable for women, the prospect for further improvements in women's relative pay is good.

Since occupational characteristics were found to play an important role in narrowing the male-female pay gap, this study also examined which occupations offer women above-average earnings and above-average employment growth rates. Not surprisingly, most of these occupations are in the managerial, professional, or technical fields. (A complete list is given in the first section of chapter 3.) The 10 most represented occupations are: teacher, registered nurse, general manager, engineer, computer programmer, computer systems analyst, accountant, engineering technician, lawyer, and physician.

Encouraging women to aspire to well-paid, high-growth jobs is particularly important, given the latest labor force projections to the year 2000. The U.S. Department of Labor expects labor demand to remain strong during the next 10 years, especially at the high end of the skills spectrum (Silvestri and Lukasiewicz 1989). The three major occupational groups requiring the highest levels of educational attainment--managerial, professional, and technical-- are projected to grow more rapidly than other occupations; more than 40 percent of all new jobs created between 1988 and 2000 will be in one of these three categories. Furthermore, the U.S. Department of Labor predicts that the demographic composition of the labor force will change dramatically between 1988 and 2000. In the past, the U.S. economy has relied heavily upon white males to work in professional, managerial, and technical occupations, but it is expected that this demographic group will represent only 15 percent of the net additions to the workforce during the next 10 years (Johnston 1987). Women, on the other hand, are expected to represent nearly two-thirds of the labor force growth between now and the year 2000, at which time 47 percent of the labor force is expected to be female.

Given these anticipated changes in the labor force, this study examined the attributes of women already employed in these well-paid, high-growth occupations. It found that these women have significantly more education and more market-oriented education than other women. Forty-four percent of these women, but only 17 percent of other women, completed college. One-third of these women majored in medical sciences and most of them are working as registered nurses. Only 8 percent of other working women majored in medical sciences. Another major difference in education was the number of mathematics courses that each group took while in high school. Over 90 percent of those women in hipaygrow occupations took algebra in high school, and almost 80 percent took geometry. On the other hand, less than three-quarters of other women took algebra in high school, and only 43 percent of these women took geometry. Finally, the educational goals of these women when they were young differed considerably. Two-thirds of those women who ended up in hipaygrow jobs wanted to complete college; only 30 percent of the other women wanted to complete college.

After reviewing the characteristics of women already in hipaygrow occupations, the next task was to examine whether today's young women are making the choices that will allow them to fill hipaygrow jobs in the future. To answer this question, the study examined the attributes of young women in 1987 and compared them to the attributes of young women 14 years earlier. In brief, women between the ages of 23 and 29 in 1987 were found to be quite different from the average woman in this age group 14 years earlier. The average amount of education completed rose slightly, from 12.7 to 13 years, but the most striking change in educational attainment was the distribution of college majors. In 1973, the largest college major for women was education, with one out of three women majoring in this field; by 1987, the largest college major had shifted to business, capturing 28 percent of the college-educated women. The other major change among young women was in their marital and fertility decisions. One-third of young women between the ages of 23 and 29 in 1987 remained single and one-half remained childless. In contrast, 14 years earlier, only 14 percent of young women in this age group remained single and two-thirds had children.

We then compared the attributes of today's young women with the attributes 14 years ago of women who currently hold well-paid, high-growth occupations. This comparison found that young women today do not have the same attributes as women in hipaygrow jobs had when they were young. Most important, only 30 percent of today's young women work in professional, managerial, and technical occupations, where most hipaygrow opportunities exist. In contrast, 50 percent of the women who end up in hipaygrow occupations in their late thirties were already in these fields when they were between the ages of 23 and 29.

Finally, this study examined the issue of intermittent labor force participation among women. Many economists have argued that the primary reason women earn less than men is because women tend to work intermittently, taking extended periods of time out of the labor force to have and rear children. These interruptions reduce women's future earnings because their skills depreciate during the time out of the labor force. Furthermore, they are not acquiring the training and work experience that lead to higher earnings in the future. Men, on the other hand, remain in the labor force throughout their adult life, gaining the necessary human capital to enhance their earnings.

To explore the issue of intermittency, this study identified those women who have worked continuously and compared their attributes to other women. We found that only 10 percent of women between the ages of 35 and 41 have worked continuously. Furthermore, their demographic characteristics are quite different from women who work intermittently. They have acquired considerably more education, averaging 16 years of education, compared to 13 years for intermittent female workers. They are also much more likely to have remained single and childless. About one-fourth of these women have never married. Among other working women, only 6 percent remain single. Half of the women who work continuously have never had children; 14 percent of other working women remain childless. Women who work continuously have acquired much more work experience than other women, even though the former tend to be about two years younger. Women who work continuously in this sample average 36 years of age and have over 16 years of work experience. In contrast, other working women are about 38 years old and have about 12 years of work experience.

In terms of earnings, this study shows that women who work continuously earn 50 percent more than women who work intermittently. Furthermore, most of this pay differential is due to differences in measured characteristics, such as education and work experience, and not differences in estimated coefficients. The mean difference in education, for example, explains almost 40 percent of the total pay differential between these two groups of women. Women do gain a wage premium, however, if they work continuously. It is estimated that the hourly pay of a woman who works intermittently would increase by 17 percent if she worked continuously. This wage premium explains 38 percent of the total pay differential between continuous and intermittent female workers. The remaining 62 percent of the pay gap can be attributed to mean differences in explanatory variables. Hence, women who work continuously experience better labor market outcomes than other female workers after productivity characteristics are taken into account, but most of their higher pay is due to productivity differences. This suggests that a factor contributing to the pay disparity between men and women is that the average male works continuously whereas the average female does not, but this factor alone does not explain the majority of the male-female pay differential.

APPENDICES

APPENDIX A

DATA SOURCES AND PREPARATION

This report uses a number of different data sources, which are described in detail here. Briefly, chapter 2 uses the University of Michigan Panel Study of Income Dynamics (PSID) to discuss the factors contributing to the increase in women's relative earnings in the 1980s. Chapter 3 uses data from the U.S. Bureau of Labor Statistics (BLS) and the U.S. Bureau of the Census to identify the set of well-paid, high-growth occupations for women, hereafter referred to as hipaygrow occupations. It then uses data from the *Dictionary of Occupational Titles* (summarized in Miller et al. 1980) and the 1980s Census to discuss the skill requirements of these jobs. The rest of chapter 3, as well as chapter 4, utilizes two cohorts of the National Longitudinal Survey (NLS), the NLS of Young Women and the NLS of Youth. The NLS of Young Women is used to assess the attributes of women in hipaygrow occupations and to estimate the earnings of intermittent female workers. Both the

NLS of Youth and the NLS of Young Women are used to make intercohort comparisons.

THE PANEL STUDY OF INCOME DYNAMICS

The original 1984 Panel Study of Income Dynamics (PSID) included 20,393 observations, but many of these people were not asked about their current work status. The PSID only asked the heads of households and their spouses or live-in partners about their current work status. Thus people who never fell into these categories between 1968 and 1984 inclusive were deleted from this study's sample, reducing it to 11,148 observations. In addition, heads of households, spouses of heads, or live-in partners of heads were not included in this analysis for any year in which they did not fall into any of these three categories.

Initially, these data were used to examine median hourly earnings for each year between 1967 and 1983. To calculate hourly earnings, a variable constructed by the PSID was employed that divides a person's annual labor income from the previous year by the total hours he or she worked that year. Anyone who had positive earnings for the previous year (approximately 75 percent of the sample) was included in the study sample. Again, people who were not heads, spouses, or live-in partners of heads had already been deleted. This left a sample that ranged in size from 2,575 in 1967 to 5,691 in 1983. The ratio of women's median hourly earnings to men's median hourly earnings was then calculated for each year between 1967 and 1983. These findings are presented in chapter 2.

Earnings equations were then estimated for 1979 and 1984 to examine why women's relative pay improved over this time period. The dependent variable in these regressions was hourly earnings from a person's current main job. Hence, this measure of hourly pay focuses upon a persons's main job, in contrast to the measure of hourly earnings just discussed above, which focuses upon total annual labor income divided by total hours worked. The regression analyses for 1979 and 1984 included all heads, spouses, or live-in partners who were at least 18 years old and were employed as civilian, nonagricultural, nonprivate-household wage and salary workers. The database included 1,964 women and 2,332 men in 1979, and 2,392 women and 2,709 men in 1984.

Most of the variables used in the regression analysis were easily recoded from the original data into dummy variables. Actual work experience, however, had a more complicated construction. The PSID asked about a person's actual work experience in 1976, including how many years a person had worked since the age of 18; how many of those years were part-time; and, for years worked part-time, what proportion of the year had been worked. Since 1976, these questions have only been asked of new household members. Thus, to obtain a person's actual work experience in 1984, these questions together with the information on a person's annual hours worked each year, had to be used. A person's actual work experience equals the sum of the following three items: (1) the number of years a person records having worked full-time when asked the original question, (2) the proportion of each year that an individual reports having worked part-time, and (3) the number of hours an individual has worked each subsequent year divided by 2000 (the PSID defines a full-time worker as a person who works at least 2,000 hours per year). Home-time is then calculated as age minus the number of years of completed schooling minus actual work experience minus five. Home-time was reassigned to zero if this calculation produced a negative number.

BUREAU OF LABOR STATISTICS DATA

The first data source used in chapter 3 of this study is an unpublished list of employment projections for detailed occupational categories, available from the U.S. Bureau of Labor Statistics (1988). It gives total employment in 1986, projected employment in the year 2000, and the percentage change in projected employment between 1986 and 2000 for detailed occupational categories. This information is used to identify the set of occupations with above-average projected employment growth rates.

An unfortunate drawback of this data source is that the BLS does not use the Standard Occupational Classification (SOC) system to delineate its set of detailed occupational categories. Instead, it uses the National Industry-Occupation Matrix. However, the SOC is used by every other major data source, including the 1980 Census, the Current Population Survey, and the two longitudinal data sources used here, the PSID and the NLS. Thus, before proceeding with this study these two classification systems had to be matched.

The BLS has attempted to match these two classification systems (1988b), but out of 580 in the National Matrix and 503 in the SOC, only 273 comparable occupations were found in both systems. This analysis examined whether this subset of 273 comparable occupations was a representative sample of SOC occupations, and found that it was significantly different from the remaining 160 occupations in the SOC classification scheme. Hence, this subset of occupations was not considered to be a representative sample of SOC occupations.

A logit model was estimated to determine whether the matched and unmatched samples of occupations were significantly different. The unit of observation was the SOC occupations. The dependent variable equaled one if the occupation was successfully matched, and zero otherwise. The independent variables were the general educational and specific skill requirements of the job, the sex composition of the job, and the average wage of the job. The results of this estimation showed that the matched occupations have significantly lower general education requirements than the unmatched occupations.

Rather than limit the analysis to an unrepresentative sample of occupations, it was decided to impute growth rates for the other SOC occupations that lacked projected employment growth data. The growth rate for each SOC occupation without this information was set equal to the growth rate for the broad occupational category that included this SOC occupation. For example, the job title "Medicine and Health Managers" does not have projected employment growth information, and thus was assigned the growth rate for Managerial and Management-Related Occupations, its broad occupational category. This imputation process appeared to be adequate, since this analysis was not interested in a precise growth rate for each occupation but wanted only to distinguish those jobs that offer women above-average employment growth rates and above-average earnings from jobs that do not.

BUREAU OF THE CENSUS DATA

The next data source used in chapter 3 of this report is the 1980 Census, which provides the average hourly earnings for women in each detailed occupation. This variable was used to ascertain which jobs had above-average earnings for women.

DICTIONARY OF OCCUPATIONAL TITLES

The final data source used in chapter 3 was the fourth edition of the *Dictionary of Occupational Titles* (summarized by Miller et al. 1980). This data source provided the general educational and specific training requirements for each job. Unfortunately, it uses the 1970 SOC classification scheme. However, the Census Bureau has developed conversion tables for the 1980 and 1970

SOC systems, which were used to add the skill information to the other occupational information discussed previously here.

THE NATIONAL LONGITUDINAL SURVEYS

The database for chapter 3 and 4 was derived from two cohorts of the National Longitudinal Survey (NLS), the NLS of Young Women and the NLS of Youth. Both of these data sets are nationally representative samples of specific age groups. In 1988, when this study began, the latest wave of the NLS of Young Women available for public use was from 1985. This survey had 3,720 respondents, or 72 percent of the original sample of 5,159 who began the survey 17 years earlier in 1968. These women were between the ages of 14 and 24 when the survey began; by 1985 they were between 31 to 41 years of age. The latest wave of the NLS of Youth that became available in early 1989 was the 1987 survey. This survey began in 1979 with 12,686 respondents. In 1987, 10,485 of these people remained in the survey. These individuals were between the ages of 14 and 21 in 1979, but were between 23 and 30 in 1987.

These surveys were selected for three reasons: (1) they are longitudinal data sets; (2) they are nationally representative samples for their age groups; and (3) they offer a broad array of questions about women's attitudes and behavior. The longitudinal nature of these data permitted a review of the earlier attributes of women who chose hipay-grow occupations later in life. This, in turn, allowed an intercohort comparison between the characteristics of young women today and the characteristics of these other young women who later chose hipaygrow jobs. In addition, these data are the only source of information that includes a woman's actual work experience as well as her attitudes toward work and family from an early age. This information enabled an examination of whether a woman's attitudes toward work and family affected her decision to work intermittently or continuously over the next 17 years of her life.

The following is a discussion of the samples and variables used from each NLS cohort. Explained in detail are the cases that were deleted from the NLS cohorts before conducting the analyses and why these deletions were made. The variables used in this study and how they were created from the original surveys are also discussed.

The NLS of Young Women

The two most important criteria for inclusion from the NLS survey were: (1) the women had to be interviewed in 1973 and 1985; and (2) they had to be between the ages of 35 and 41 in 1985. This reduced the study sample to 2,522 respondents, down from 5,159 who began the survey in 1968. Each criterion contributed about half of the losses in respondents. The sample was restricted to those interviewed in 1985, so that the women's characteristics could be examined from the latest survey available at the beginning of this study. The sample was further restricted to those who were also interviewed in 1973, so that the characteristics of these women when they were considerably younger could be examined and compared to the characteristics of young women in the NLS of Youth in 1987. The ages were restricted so that these women would have the same range of ages in 1973 as the women in the NLS of Youth in 1987.

Three additional restrictions, made to facilitate the analyses, further restricted the sample to 1,548. First, any respondent who did not report either her total family income or her labor income in 1985 was deleted from the sample. Second, any respondent who did not indicate whether or not she lived in an SMSA in 1985 was deleted. Finally, anyone who was self-employed in 1985 was deleted. Family income other than a woman's labor income is a key factor for predicting whether or not a woman will work. As other family income increases, the likelihood that a woman will work decreases. Hence, this analysis deleted those cases without this information. Many cases did not have information about the size of their Standard Metropolitan Statistical Area (SMSA) to protect the confidentiality of the respondent's identity. But living in an SMSA influences whether or not a person works, how much he or she earns, and the type of occupation he or she selects. Thus, this variable was used throughout this analysis, and individuals without this information were deleted from the sample. Finally, the NLS does not ask people who are self-employed how much they earn from this line of work. Thus, it was not possible to determine whether such businesses give them positive earnings, negative earnings, or no earnings. Since earnings are examined throughout this study, self-employed people were also deleted.

Most of the variables used in the study were taken directly from the 1985 (or 1973) NLS of Young Women. Three variables, however, had to be constructed from data contained in several years of the NLS. These were the number of years of education completed, the type of college major, and the number of years of actual work experience. The first two of these variables, education and college major, were the simplest to construct since questions about these attributes were included in every questionnaire conducted by the NLS of Young Women. The amount of completed education in 1985 was set equal to the highest value given in any survey year. The type of college major was set equal to the last college major ever recorded. The values used to code college major changed, however, during the course of this survey. The later coding scheme was converted to the earlier one so that the data had a consistent set of values for college major.

A woman's actual work experience was much more difficult to calculate than originally expected. During the first 11 years of the NLS of Young Women, the survey asked respondents how many weeks they had worked the previous calendar year. This approach was sufficient for constructing a woman's work experience during the first 6 years of the survey, when the survey was conducted annually. After 1973, however, the survey tended to be administered every 2 years, but no question was asked about a woman's work experience during those intervening years. For example, no survey was administered in 1974, but the 1975 survey only asked about work experience in 1974. The NLS of Young Women never recorded the number of weeks worked in 1973. The same omission was made for work experience in 1975. Thus, by 1978 two years, 1973 and 1975, were unaccounted for in terms of a woman's work experience. Hence, a question was added to the 1978 survey that asked women how many years, during the past five years, they had worked at least six months. This question could be used to replace the missing work experience information for 1973 and 1975, but it meant that work experience could not be measured by weeks worked per year. Instead, the only consistent measure of work experience available for the entire 17 years of the survey between 1968 and 1985 was the number of years a respondent worked at least six months. After 1978, the NLS of Young Women revised its questionnaire so that respondents were asked how many weeks they had worked since the last interview. Thus, if two years had passed since the last interview, two years of work experience information were collected.

It was also necessary to determine whether or not a woman had worked continuously. To construct this variable, this analysis started with a woman's age in 1985 and subtracted the number of years of formal education she had completed. Then the number of years she had worked at least six months was subtracted. Finally, five was subtracted, since people generally start school at age five. This final number is a variable in the analysis called *home-time*, which represents the number of years an individual is not working or going to school. If this is positive, the woman is considered an intermittent worker. If this number is equal to zero (or negative), then she is said to have worked continuously.

The one set of unconventional variables included in this study are the attitudinal variables about work and family from the NLS. The first two of these variables included in the study asked respondents about their educational goals and future plans at age 35. The other study variable asked women whether they believe that a woman's place is in the home rather than the office. The first two questions were asked in 1968, when the girls are between the ages of 14 and 24. The latter question was not asked until 1973, when the girls are between the ages of 19 and 29.

The exact wording of these attitudinal variables is given here, since they are not readily available nor widely used in other labor market studies. The way in which these variables were recoded for this analysis is also describe. The first question asked: "What would you like to be doing when you are 35 years old?" The answers to this question are categorized as (1) planned to be working, (2) planned to be married and raising a family, (3) don't know, or (4) other. If the respondents planned to be working, the survey asked them what kind of work they desired. The first variable was recoded into a dummy variable that equaled one if the respondent said she would like to be working at age 35, and zero otherwise. The second variable, the desired occupation at age 35, was also recoded into a dummy variable that equaled one if the respondent desired a professional or managerial occupation, and zero otherwise. The second question asked: "How much education would you like to get?" The answers were allowed to range from 8 to 18 years of education. This variable was not recoded for this analysis. The third question asked respondents to indicate their agreement with the statement: "A woman's place is in the home, not in the office or shop." They could answer: (1) strongly agree, (2) agree, (3) disagree, (4) strongly disagree, or (5) undecided. This variable was recoded into a dummy variable that equals one if the woman answered (1) or (2), and zero if she answered (3), (4), or (5).

The NLS of Youth

The original National Longitudinal Survey of Youth database contained 12,686 observations. From this data, we extracted those individuals who were female and between the ages of 23 and 29 years old in 1987. They also had to have a positive individual weight assigned by the survey, which was used to transform the sample into a nationally representative sample of this age group. This left 4,748 observations. The only variables that we constructed were the number of mathematics courses taken in high school and the work experience variables. The number of mathematics courses taken in algebra, geometry, trigonometry, and calculus was determined by examining a person's high school transcripts, which were coded onto the NLS of Youth. The total number of semesters completed in each of the subjects just listed was calculated for each person. Each semester was counted as half a year. Thus, if a woman took three semesters of algebra, for example, she was accorded 1.5 years of algebra. An individual's work experience is equal to the number of years a person worked at least six months from 1981 to 1986.

APPENDIX B

THEORETICAL MODELS

BIVARIATE PROBIT MODEL FOR CHAPTER 3

Women who select a hipaygrow job are, in fact, making two decisions. The first decision is whether or not to work. The second decision is whether or not to select a hipaygrow job. These two decisions are modeled in the following manner, respectively:

$$I_{1i} = A_1'Z_{1i} + v_{1i} \qquad \text{(B.1)}$$

$$I_{2i} = A_2'Z_{2i} + v_{2i} \qquad \text{(B.2)}$$

where: the I_{ji}s represent the unobserved indexes of utility that the individual uses to make j decisions ($j = 1, 2$); the Z_{ji}s are K_j x 1 vectors of explanatory variables; the A_js are K_j x 1 vectors of unknown parameters; the v_{ji}s are assumed to be $N(0, 1)$ with $cov(v_1, v_2) = \rho$.

Although the I_{js}s are unobserved, two dummy variables can be defined in the following way:

$$D_1 = 1 \text{ if } I_1 > 0$$
$$D_1 = 0 \text{ if } I_1 < 0 \tag{B.3}$$

$$D_2 = 1 \text{ if } I_2 > 0$$
$$D_2 = 0 \text{ if } I_2 < 0 \tag{B.4}$$

D_1 is always observed, but D_2 is observed if and only if D_1
is equal to 1. In other words, individuals make two
simultaneous decisions, whether or not to work and
whether or not to take a hipaygrow job. There is partial
observability, however, since the outcome of the second
decision is unknown if the woman decides to stay home.

These two decision equations can then be estimated with
the dummy variables as the dependent variables. A full
information maximum-likelihood function can be used,
which depends upon the bivariate normal distribution.
Maximizing this function produces consistent estimates of
A_1, A_2, and ρ.

BIVARIATE PROBIT MODEL FOR CHAPTER 4

Chapter 4 estimates earnings equations for intermittent and
continuous female workers. As explained in the chapter,

selectivity biases may occur, since the underlying decision processes are ignored when estimating wage equations using ordinary least-squares regression analysis. To correct for these possible selection biases, a bivariate probit selectivity model was employed. In this model, an individual makes two decisions: whether or not to work continuously and whether or not to work currently. I assumed that the two decisions could be modeled in the following manner, respectively:

$$I_{1i} = A_1, Z_{1i} + v_{1i} \tag{B.5}$$

$$I_{2i} = A_2, Z_{2i} + v_{2i} \tag{B.6}$$

where: the I_{ji}s represent the unobserved indexes of utility that the individual uses to make j decisions ($j = 1, 2$); the Z_{ji}s are $K_j \times 1$ vectors of explanatory variables; the A_js are $K_j \times 1$ vectors of unknown parameters; the v_{ji}s are assumed to be $N(0, 1,)$ with $cov(v_1, v_2) = \rho$.

Although the I_{ji}s are unobserved, two dummy variables can be defined in the following way.

$$D_1 = 1 \text{ if } I_1 > 0$$
$$\tag{B.7}$$
$$D_1 = 0 \text{ if } I_1 < 0$$

$$D_2 = 1 \text{ if } I_2 > 0$$
$$\tag{B.8}$$
$$D_2 = 0 \text{ if } I_2 < 0$$

In other words, individuals make two sequential decisions. First, they decide whether or not to work continuously. Then they decide whether or not to select a paid job currently. Thus, there is full information on the outcomes of these two decision rules, giving four distinct cells: (1) a woman could choose to work continuously and to work currently, (2) a woman could decide not to work continuously, but choose to work currently, (3) a woman could choose to work continuously in the past, but decide not to work currently, and (4) a woman could decide not to work continuously or currently.

This analysis was interested in estimating earnings equations for the first two groups of women after correcting for this double-selection. Thus, it was assumed that the earnings of women for the relevant decisions combinations could be described by the following equations.

$$\ln w_{1i} = B_1'X_{1i} + u_{1i} \text{ iff } i \in S_1 \quad (B.9)$$

$$\ln w_{2i} = B_2'X_{2i} + u_{2i} \text{ iff } i \in S_2, \quad (B.10)$$

where:

$$S_1 = \{i \mid I_1 > 0, I_2 >\} \quad (B.11)$$

$$S_2 = \{i \mid I_1 > 0, I_2 >\} \quad (B.12)$$

The w_{hi} represents earnings for group h ($h=1, 2$); the B_hs are $L_h \times 1$ vectors of unknown population parameters; the X_{hi}s are $L_h \times 1$ vectors of explanatory variables; the u_{hi}s are identically and independently distributed normal variates. However, each u_{hi} is jointly distributed with each v_{ji}, such that

$$cov(u_{hi}, v_{ji}) = \rho_{hj}. \tag{B.13}$$

The aforementioned earnings equation define population earnings. A regression function for each subsample may be written as:

$$\ln w_{1i} = B_1 , X_{1i} + a_1 \lambda_{1i} + a_2 \lambda_{2i} + Y_{3i}$$

$$\ln w_{2i} = B_2 , X_{2i} + a_3 \lambda_{3i} + a_4 \lambda_{4i} + Y_{4i}$$

$$\tag{B.14}$$

where the four λs constitute the double selection analogs of the inverse Mills' ratio that arises in the context of single selection (for a detailed discussion, see Tunali 1986).

A two-step procedure can be used to estimate these equations. It consists of estimating the two decision equations previously described using a full information maximum-likelihood function, which depends upon the bivariate normal distribution. Maximizing this function produces consistent estimates of A_1, A_2, and ρ. These estimates can then be used to compute consistent estimates of the λs. Inserting these two into the appropriate earnings equations and estimating these equations using ordinary least squares (OLS) produces consistent estimates of B_1 and B_2.

REFERENCES

Bernstein, Aaron. 1988. "So You Think You've Come a Long Way, Baby?" *Business Week*, Feb. 29, 1988, 48.

Blackburn, McKinley, David Bloom, and Richard B. Freeman. 1990. "Why Has the Economic Position of Less-Skilled Male Workers Deteriorated in the United States?" In *A Future of Lousy Jobs*, edited by Gary Burtless. Washington, D.C.: Brookings Institution.

Blau, Francine D., and Andrea H. Beller. 1988. "Trends in Earnings Differentials by Gender, 1971-1981." *Industrial and Labor Relations Review* 41(4): 513-29.

Blinder, Alan S. 1973. "Wage Discrimination: Reduced Form and Structural Estimates." *Journal of Human Resources* 8(4): 436-55.

Bound, John, and George Johnson. 1988. "Changes in the Structure of Wages during the 1980s: An Evaluation of Alternative Explanations." Working Paper 2983, Cambridge, Mass. National Bureau of Economic Research.

Cain, Glen G. 1986. "The Economic Analysis of Labor Market Discrimination: A Survey." In *Handbook of Labor Economics*, edited by Orley Ashenfelter and Richard Layard, 693-785. Amsterdam: Elsevier Science Publishers.

Corcoran, Mary, and Greg J. Duncan. 1979. "Work History, Labor Force Attachment, and Earnings Differences between the Races and Sexes." *Journal of Human Resources* 14: 3-19.

Duncan, Gregory M., and Duane E. Leigh. 1980. "Wage Determination in the Union and Nonunion Sectors: A Sample Selectivity Approach." *Industrial and Labor Relations Review* 34: 24-35.

Fuchs, Victor R. 1988. *Women's Quest for Economic Equality*. Cambridge, Mass: Harvard University Press.

Fullerton, Howard N., Jr. 1989. "New Labor Force Projections, Spanning 1988 to 2000." *Monthly Labor Review* 112(11): 3-12.

Goldin, Claudia, and Solomon Polachek. 1987. "Residual Differences by Sex: Perspectives on the Gender Gap in

Earnings." *American Economic Review* 77 (May): 143-151.

Gronau, Reuben. 1974. "Wage Comparisons--A Selectivity Bias." *Journal of Political Economy* 82(6): 1119-43.

Heckman, James J. 1979. "Sample Selection Bias as a Specification Error." *Econometrica* 47 (January): 153-61.

Johnston, William B. 1987. *Workforce 2000*. Indiana: Hudson Institute.

Kosters, Marvin H. 1989. "Wages and Demographics." Paper presented at conference on "Wages in the 1980s," American Enterprise Institute, Washington, D.C., November.

Levy, Frank. 1988. "Income, Families, and Living Standards." In *American Living Standards: Threats and Challenges*, edited by Robert E. Litan. Washington, D.C.: Brookings Institution: 108-153.

Miller, Ann R., Donald J. Treiman, Pamela S. Cain, and Patricia A. Roos, eds. 1980. *Work, Jobs, and Occupations: A Critical Review of the Dictionary of Occupational Titles*. Washington, D.C.: National Academy Press.

Mincer, Jacob, and Solomon Polachek. 1974. "Family Investments in Human Capital: Earnings of Women."

Journal of Political Economy 82 (March/April): S76-S108.

Murphy, Kevin, and Finis Welch. 1988. "The Structure of Wages." Photocopy.

Oaxaca, Ronald. 1973. "Male-Female Wage Differentials in Urban Labor Markets." *International Economic Review* 14(3): 693-709.

Reimers, Cordelia W. 1983. "Labor Market Discrimination against Hispanic and Black Men." *Review of Economics and Statistics* 65 (4): 570-79.

Silvestri, George, and John Lukasiewicz. 1989. "Projections of Occupational Employment, 1988-2000." *Monthly Labor Review*, 112(11): 42-65.

Smith, James P., and Michael P. Ward. 1984. "Women's Wages and Work in the Twentieth Century." Los Angeles, Calif.: Rand Publication Series.

Tunali, Insan. 1986. "A General Structure for Models of Double-Selection and an Application to a Joint Migration/Earnings Process with Re-Migration." In *Research in Labor Economics*, vol. 8, part B, edited by Ronald G. Ehrenberg, 235-84. Greenwich, Conn: JAI Press.

U.S. Bureau of Labor Statistics. 1988a. "Total Employment by Occupation: 1986 and 2000 Projected, Matrix-

I." U.S. Bureau of Labor Statistics, Washington, D.C. Photocopy.

U.S. Bureau of Labor Statistics. 1988b. *Occupational Projections and Training Data*, Bulletin 2301. Washington, D.C.: U.S. Government Printing Ofice.

U.S. Bureau of Labor Statistics. 1989. *Employment and Earnings*, vol. 36. Washington, D.C.: U.S. Government Printing Office, January.

U.S. Bureau of the Census. 1972. *1970 Occupation by Industry*. PC(2)-7C Subject Report. Washington, D.C.: U.S. Government Printing Office.

U.S. Bureau of the Census. 1987. "Male-Female Differences in Work Experience, Occupation, and Earnings: 1984." *Current Population Reports*, Series P-70, No. 10. Washington, D.C.: U.S. Government Printing Office.

U.S. Bureau of the Census. 1987. *Statistical Abstract of the United States: 1988*. Washington, D.C.: U.S. Government Printing Office, 1987.

U.S. Department of Labor. 1972. *Handbook for Analyzing Jobs*. Washington, D.C.: U.S. Government Printing Office.

Vroman, Wayne. 1989. "Industrial Change and Black Men's Relative Earnings." Urban Institute Working Paper, Washington, D.C.: Urban Institute.